AF506012

Banking Reform in India and China

Banking Reform in
India and China

By

Lawrence Sáez

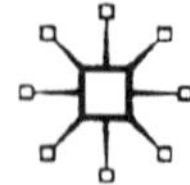

BANKING REFORM IN INDIA AND CHINA
© Lawrence Sáez, 2004.

First published 2004 by
PALGRAVE MACMILLAN™
175 Fifth Avenue, New York, N.Y. 10010 and
Houndmills, Basingstoke, Hampshire, England RG21 6XS
Companies and representatives throughout the world

Palgrave Macmillan is the global academic imprint of the Palgrave Macmillan division of St. Martin's Press, LLC and of Palgrave Macmillan Ltd. Macmillan® is a registered trademark in the United States, United Kingdom and other countries. Palgrave is a registered trademark in the European Union and other countries.

ISBN 0–312–23935–1 hardback

Library of Congress Cataloging-in-Publication Data
Sáez, Lawrence, 1965–
    Banking reform in India and China / by Lawrence Sáez.
        p. cm.
    Includes bibliographical references and index.
    ISBN 0–312–23935–1
     1. Banks and banking—India. 2. Banks and banking—China. I. Title.

HG3284.S23 2003
332.1'0951—dc21   2003049851

A catalogue record for this book is available from the British Library.

Design by Newgen Imaging Systems (P) Ltd., Chennai, India.

First edition: January, 2004
10 9 8 7 6 5 4 3 2 1

Printed in the United States of America.

For Jackson Ming Sáez

Contents

Acknowledgments

This book is an attempt at a comparative, critical study of India and China's banking reforms. The bulk of this book was written while I was an assistant research political scientist at the Institute of East Asian Studies at the University of California at Berkeley. During my stay at Berkeley, I was also a visiting scholar at the Center for South Asia Studies. I wish to thank my hosts, the late Raba Gunasekara, Joan Kask, and Steven Poulos, for their common sense.

Final portions of the manuscript were completed while I was a visiting research fellow at the Center for International Studies at the London School of Economics. As such, Pam Hodges deserves special accolades. During my academic visit to England, I was also a senior associate member at St. Antony's College and a visiting South Asia fellow at Queen Elizabeth House, both at the University of Oxford. Accordingly I am indebted to my kind sponsors both at Oxford and at the LSE, Nandini Gooptu, Barbara Harriss-White, John Kent, Margot Light, and David Washbrook. I also wish to thank the Asia Pacific team at Oxford Analytica. As a contributing writer in this institution I wish to thank Euan Graham, Graham Hutchings, and Scott Urban.

This book builds upon some of the comparative work that I developed in my Ph.D. dissertation in the Political Science Department at the University of Chicago. As a graduate student, Professors Lloyd and Susanne Rudolph encouraged me to further the comparative research of economic liberalization in India and China. For better or worse I have followed their advise to the best of my ability.

Over the years I have benefited from discussions with many scholars and friends whose contribution to this volume are important but cannot often be singled out individually. Nevertheless I want to make special mention of Montek Singh Ahluwalia, Pradipta Bagchi, Sumon Bhaumik, Delia Boylan, K.B. Chandrashekhar, Meghnad Desai, Rafiq Dossani, Leslie Elliot-Armijo, Stephen Green, Santanu Gupta, M. Kabir Hassan, Athar Hussain, Peter

Katzenstein, Anne Krueger, Yidan Li, Justin Lin, Xin Ma, Joydeep Mukherji, Brian Murray, Yingyi Qian, Arthur Rubinoff, Matthew Rudolph, Kaja Sehrt, Nirvikar Singh, Kannan Srinivansan, T.N. Srinivasan, Kellee Tsai, Linda Yueh, and Liu Yunzhong.

During my research, I have also had the opportunity to talk informally with many government officials who have played a direct role in the formulation of banking policy. Among Chinese government officials I especially wish to acknowledge: Li Ruogu, the assistant governor of the People's Bank of China; Xie Ping, the director general of the Department of Research of the People's Bank of China; Gao Xiqing, the deputy chairman of the China Securities Regulatory Commission; Lou Jiwei, vice minister of the Ministry of Finance; Cao Yushu, the vice chairman and secretary general of the State Economic and Trade Commission for their candor. Many Indian government officials have also offered their candid opinions to me. They include Finance Minister Yashwant Sinha; Finance Minister Palaniappan Chidambaram, L.K. Singhvi, senior executive director of the Security and Exchange Board of India; Sudhakar Rao, minister of Economic Affairs; and Shankar Acharya, chief economic advisor to the Ministry of Finance.

Anthony Wahl at Palgrave guided me through the publication process, both in its exhilarating and dispiriting moments. Over the years I have learnt that editing a book manuscript is an art that cannot be completely mastered by any single individual. I owe special thanks to my former colleagues at Asian Survey, Bonnie Dehler and Carl Freire, for initiating me into the obtuse world of copyediting. As this book will show, though, errors of fact and analysis will creep into any manuscript. Although I am willing to share the blame, I alone am responsible for the accuracy of fact and correctness of interpretation as presented herein. Thanks also go to Joyce Kallgren and Lowell Dittmer for adding candid perspectives on academic life.

Since this book has developed over the course of several years, some of my earlier essays foreshadowed some of the arguments in it. Some of the ideas contained in this book have appeared in earlier versions in "The Political Economy of Banking Reform in India and China," *International Journal of Finance and Economics*, Vol. 6, No. 3 (July 2001), and "The Deregulation of State-Owned Enterprises in India and China," *Comparative Economic Studies*, Vol. 43, No. 3 (Fall 2001).

Special acknowledgment must be made to my wife, Joy Yang, for tolerating her annoying husband. This book is dedicated to my son, Jackson Ming Sáez, who has provided me with infinite happiness since his birth and who has developed much more successfully than this book.

CHAPTER 1

Introduction

In an era of growing capital mobility and the liberalization of capital markets, the goal of financial liberalization was among the most pressing issues for policymakers in the 1990s. The expansion, diversification, and modernization of financial services have emphasized greater participation in the global economy. At the same time, financial liberalization has presented new challenges. Although lower barriers to entry have attracted transnational capital flows, they have also introduced a new degree of uncertainty and volatility in the domestic economies of emerging markets.

The interest in financial liberalization, though, has been reoriented as a result of the 1997 East Asian financial crisis. Prior to the crisis, Indonesia, Thailand, South Korea, and Malaysia were seen as models of financial liberalization (Chant and Pangestu, 1994; Cho and Khatkhate, 1989; World Bank, 1993). Since then, other emerging markets have not had an alternative model to the East Asian one. In 1997, some of the most dynamic economies of the world experienced a devastating financial crisis. The East Asian financial crisis showed that the progress and outcomes of financial liberalization had widespread repercussions and lingering effects in other parts of the world. Analysts have attempted to explain how and why the financial crisis occurred at all. The financial crisis revealed that a growing economy could not be sustained with a weak banking infrastructure.

It is essential to understand the complexities of banking sector reforms because the banking sector in developing countries is particularly vulnerable as economies are opened to international financial markets. The fragility of the banking system has raised a new consensus that financial sector stability is a precursor to and is essential to long-term economic growth and poverty reduction in developing countries (World Bank, 2001: 76). Moreover, the lingering weaknesses in the banking sector have resulted in costly bailouts. Curiously, the literature that emerged after the East Asian financial crisis has not examined how another financial crisis of this magnitude can be averted. Hence the issue of banking reform needs to move toward the forefront of economic development.

The two largest developing countries in the world, India and China, are currently experiencing some of the symptoms that bedeviled Malaysia, Thailand, and Indonesia prior to their respective financial crises. Some estimates calculate that bank debts and nonperforming loans of China's state-owned banks amount to nearly 30 percent of China's gross domestic product. Similarly India is also facing a banking crisis. Given the substantial presence of American and European firms in China and India, a financial crisis could have devastating repercussions globally.

Although clearly the most immediate element of banking reform concerns the problems of nonperforming assets held by Indian and Chinese state-owned banks, it is by no means the only exclusive problem facing this industry. Financial and capital market reforms are also in the process of implementation. Like efforts in the banking sector, these reforms have been carried out with greater speed than either country has been able to sustain institutionally. In addition, the friction between domestic institutions and international financial regulations is a further challenge to emerging market economies. Likewise, studies of financial regulations (Brownbridge, 2002; Brownbridge and Kirkpatrick, 2000; Caprio et al., 2001; Mansoob Murshed and Subagjo, 2002) have argued that there are intractable institutional impediments to adequate prudential regulation in developing countries.

In order to reduce the likelihood of financial crises, the emerging financial architecture must be consistent with the variety of domestic frameworks and should take into account some critical peculiarities of developing economies. Thus, in this book, I will frame my discussion about banking reform from a number of perspectives, including corporate governance, asset management, and central bank independence.

1.1   A Comparison of China and India

The comparison of reform in China and India should be interesting to students of international political economy for several reasons. China and India have had similar developmental patterns. Some of the development patterns fostered some landmark studies in comparative economics. Alexander Eckstein (1954, 1955a,b) and Rosen (1954) provided one of the most ambitious early efforts to evaluate China's political economy. Wilfred

Malenbaum (1956) undertook another such effort. In Malenbaum's study, the key defining variable in India and China's developmental objectives was the underlying logic between the different approaches to rapid economic growth. According to Malenbaum, China's Soviet-model rapid industrialization program was "power-oriented," namely geared for the purpose of cementing the Communist Party's centralized control over the country. In contrast, India's developmental planning was portrayed by Malenbaum as being "welfare-oriented," namely geared toward improving the average Indians' overall welfare.

Subsequent comparative studies of India and China (Bandyopadhyaya, 1976; Bardhan, 1971; Bhalla, 1992; Lateef, 1976; Raj, 1983; Rosen, 1992; Srinivas, 2002; Swamy, 1973) have tended to focus on the differences in agricultural and industrial output. For instance, Drèze and Saran (1993) and Sen (1995) have examined the differences in social conditions. At this stage, China and India's development paths had diverged considerably, and some authors (Weisskopf, 1975) attempted to evaluate the impact that this divergence had on economic development.

The adoption of neoliberal macroeconomic reforms in the developing world has revived the scholarship in comparative economics. Although China's first stage of reforms began in 1978 and India undertook some gradual liberalization in the mid-1980s, China and India's reform efforts were overshadowed by economic and political transition in Eastern Europe and Latin America. The neglect of studies on China and India's economic reforms may be explained because unlike other transition economies in Eastern Europe and Latin America, China and India opted to adopt gradual economic reforms. Although China and India's approach to economic reform has been quite similar, their outcome has been radically different. China has reported unprecedented levels of continuous economic growth. Moreover, China is the world's second largest recipient of foreign direct investment. In contrast, while pursuing similar economic reforms, India has experienced moderate levels of economic growth and has attracted modest levels of foreign direct investment.

The similarities of the trajectories of the nature of economic reforms in China and India have given rise to a new wave of literature on comparative political economy. The new literature (Bhalla, 1995; Cable, 1995; Srinivasan, 1990) has gradually shifted attention away from purely internal developmental differences between India and China toward an examination of external factors and the challenges that these two countries face in light of growing global integration. Some comparative studies (Cable, 1995; Dethier, 2000; Echeverri-Gent and Müller, 1990; LaCroix et al., 1999) have highlighted size as a critical factor linking these two countries. Others (Lal, 1995; Rosen, 1990; Srinivasan, 1987) have instead emphasized the critical differences in the timing and speed of economic reform.

In contrast, China and India have experienced different outcomes from their respective economic reforms. To date, China's indicators of macroeconomic growth have far surpassed those of India, particularly in terms of GDP growth and growth in per capita income. Consequently, some of the comparative literature on economic growth has attempted to uncover the lessons that India can learn from China (Dzever and Jaussaud, 1999; Sáez, 1998).

Moreover, the literature on comparative economic reform has not paid attention to the effects of reform on the financial sector. As Srinavasan's (1987: 151) comparative analysis of economic liberalization in India and China showed "sectors in which resource use is particularly inefficient in the preliberalization era and in which flexible resource reallocation is possible can achieve impressive rates of growth as resource use efficiency improves with liberalization." However, Srinavasan explained that the boost to growth is not indefinite. According to Srinavasan, "once such efficiency gains are exhausted, further growth will depend on factor accumulation and more importantly on technical progress."

Empirical studies of the relationship between concentration in the banking sector and economic growth (Deidda and Fattouh, 2002) have shown that banking concentration is detrimental to economic growth due to the duplication of fixed costs. According to Deidda and Fattouh, banking concentration is also negatively correlated with industrial growth in low-income countries. In this book I will argue that India's liberalization of the financial sector will increase internal and external competition, thus leading to a corresponding increase in the technical progress necessary to sustain long-term rates of economic growth.

China's spectacular macroeconomic performance has come at the cost of neglecting its banking infrastructure. Paradoxically, India's comparatively solid banking infrastructure has not prevented it from continuing to have a sluggish macroeconomic performance. This book will suggest that the absence of optimal financial sector reform will inhibit growth in other areas of the economy and could undermine the reform effort altogether. It will argue that China's banking system exemplifies a case of progressive collapse, whereby the structural foundations of China's banking system is eroding imperceptibly until they collapse under their own weight.

The potentially imminent collapse of China's banking system is deceiving for a number of factors. China's growth has been linked to an extraordinary growth rate in exports. Foreign sector participation in China's exports has been crucial to its success. However, the East Asian financial crisis forced China to reassess its reliance on export-led growth since it had its first decline in foreign direct investment receipts. Hence, China's long-term growth is likely to stem from the performance of its domestic industries.

China's future need to switch its pattern of growth toward domestic industries faces a critical challenge; namely that the state-owned sector is hopelessly inefficient and remains obdurately opposed to change. State-owned companies employ the largest section of society, but lags behind collectively owned industries in the proportion of overall industrial output. Collectively owned industries continue to play a significant part in China's industrial output, but its success is threatened by a lack of access to credit. For this reason, the successful reform of China's state-owned industries is intimately tied to the ability of banks to provide credit to those industries most capable of growth.

In contrast, India's modest growth in exports has forced domestic industries to seek alternative sources of equity. This is a lesson that has been most optimally learnt by India's fastest growing sector, namely the telecommunications and information technology industries. These industries are also India's net foreign exchange earners. According to estimates by the National Association of Software and Service Companies (NASSCOM), the software development and information technology outsourcing accounts for nearly 27 percent of India's exports. These incentives have prompted the banking sector to adapt to its needs, rather than the other way around. As analyzed by Mukherji (1999), the ability to raise long-term debt has diminished the vulnerability of Indian companies to short-term liquidity crises.

This book will uncover some the dynamics of banking reform in China and India. The book initially details the institutional framework of banking in China and India. The book will show that the basic institutional settings do not entirely appear to help explain the differences in outcomes. Therefore, the book seeks to clarify the intricate issue of banking and financial services reform. Here I have identified three themes in banking and financial services reform: corporate governance, financial deregulation, and central bank independence. I will show how these three seemingly unrelated themes interconnect to support a lasting banking infrastructure.

There are many excellent books that have studied various aspects of the banking systems in China and India. One of the pioneering examinations of China's modern banking system is Byrd (1983). There are many subsequent studies that have traced the current development of China's banking system. I think that students of China's banking system will certainly benefit from Girardin (1997) and Tong (1999, 2002).

Although subject to comparatively less scholarly scrutiny, there have also been some excellent works on India's banking system. Although hopelessly outdated, one of the most influential analyses of India's banking system is John Maynard Keynes's (1913) study of banking in pre-Independence India. Obviously, much has changed in India's banking system since then. Unfortunately, contemporary works on India's banking system have tended to concentrate narrowly on its institutional development. An exception to this trend is a very perceptive critical study of India's banking reform undertaken by Raje (2000).

This book aims to build upon these fine studies. This book offers some novel assessments of key aspects of the banking system of these two countries. First, the book updates some of the recent developments in the form of the banking system since China's enactment of the four basic banking laws in 1995 and since the release of India's first Narasimha committee report. This book is also unique in that it offers the first comparative look at banking reform. Viewed in isolation, single-country banking reform studies do not offer an effective sense of policy convergence. As this book will show, China and India's banking systems are moving in the direction of having a fully developed commercial banking system in conjunction with capital and money markets.

While the book focuses on these two countries, it offers general insights into other low-income countries that have yet to initiate substantial financial liberalization. By drawing on the comparisons between developments in the banking systems in China and India, this book expects to offer a more holistic perspective of the banking system in emerging markets.

This book will focus on the efforts that India and China have taken to reform their banking system. There are many approaches that can be taken to accomplish this task. Here I have chosen to focus on the area of the current weakness of state-owned banks' loan portfolios. As I hinted at the beginning of this chapter, though, the issue of nonperforming assets may lead to the unraveling of China's export-led growth.

Banking reform in India and China seeks to extend the analysis of banking reform in India and China beyond the narrow confines of the issue of nonperforming assets in state-owned banks. In their study of banking regulation, Dewatripont and Tirole (1993) linked the optimal corporate governance structure of banks with the structure of the bank's liabilities. They argued that ex ante regulation, in the form of capital adequacy requirements and limits to deposit expansion, can lower the incentive to collude by large debt holders and management, to pilfer depositors and deposit insurers. Using a model of the efficient governance structure of firms, they also proposed a series of ex post regulatory interference to force banking management to act safely. This model, though, does not properly address situations where bank managers, regulators, and debt holders act in collusion and where there is also a lack of private ex post remedies. Therefore, this book will argue that, in these perverse circumstances, reforms in capital markets can improve the corporate governance and, in turn, the performance of banks.

Moreover, in economies where the banking sector is highly regulated by the state, the performance of banks is intricately linked to macroeconomic central bank measures. As such, the book will examine the efforts that Indian and Chinese central bankers have undertaken to improve the performance of weak banks. I will argue that the degree of central bank independence closely circumscribes the range of policy options available to central banks. The outcomes of these options manifest themselves in the way in which Indian and Chinese central banks have asserted themselves on the internal operations of banks.

The experience of China and India is also interesting because they have faced the option of rehabilitating the existing state-owned commercial banks or allowing the development of a parallel banking system to emerge. China and India's experiences are of particular theoretical importance because they offer insight into other low-income countries that have yet to initiate substantial financial liberalization. Moreover, I have chosen this parameter because nonperforming assets and bad loans are the most critical element in India and China's banking system. As such I will examine whether China's attempt to rehabilitate its state-owned banks has proven to be more successful at reducing nonperforming assets than India's effort to allow new entrants into the banking sector. The conclusions reached here are not necessarily country-specific. Other emerging markets are facing similar challenges in their attempts to build a sound financial system.

Previous analyses of economic reform have shown that some countries have pursued certain types of economic reform with reference to the ability to overcome initial bureaucratic resistance to reform (Geddes, 1991; Krueger, 1986). However, economic reform poses a puzzle to students of comparative politics because some countries have pursued a range of reforms across different sectors of the economy. For instance, in some countries privatization of SOEs may be more aggressively carried out in the energy field than in telecommunications. While this book only concentrates on the cases of India and China, the utility model shown in chapter 4 offers general insight into other low-income emerging markets that have yet to initiate substantial financial liberalization. My heuristic explanation suggests that different countries opt for different levels of reform based on the state's market share in a given industry. I will argue that industry concentration in the state sector is the principal variable for the differing approaches to banking reform.

1.2 Further Theoretical Considerations

Financial sector liberalization often entails the dismantling of interest rate ceilings and capital market convertibility. The projected benefits of financial sector liberalization include efficient credit allocation, increased financial intermediation, and financial deepening. The evidence from China and India provides mixed proof for this developmental trajectory. An indicator of financial intermediation (the ratio of currency to broad money) and an indicator of financial deepening (the ratio of broad money to GDP) shows that since the 1990s, China and India have shown divergent policy outcomes in financial intermediation and financial deepening. (See tables 1.1 and 1.2.)

Table 1.1 shows that the indicator of financial intermediation (the ratio of currency to broad money) suggests an increase in monetization in India and a steady decline in China. However, table 1.2 provides the surprising finding that the reverse trend holds true for the indicator of financial deepening (the ratio of broad money to GDP). The second indicator suggests that financial deepening has increased steadily in China while it has remained constant in India.

Table 1.1 Ratio of currency to broad money in China and India, 1990–1999

	1990	1991	1992	1993	1994	1995	1996	1997	1998	1999
China	0.38	0.35	0.37	0.34	0.34	0.31	0.29	0.27	0.26	0.26
India	0.59	0.57	0.58	0.59	0.56	0.60	0.60	0.60	0.61	0.62

Source: International Monetary Fund, 2000.

Table 1.2 Ratio of broad money to gross domestic product, 1990–1999

	1990	1991	1992	1993	1994	1995	1996	1997	1998	1999
China	0.38	0.42	0.45	0.49	0.46	0.44	0.45	0.51	0.54	0.62
India	0.16	0.17	0.16	0.15	0.15	0.16	0.16	0.16	0.15	0.16

Source: International Monetary Fund, 2000.

The anomalies found in China and India with respect to financial intermediation and financial deepening apply to other theoretical aspects of financial liberalization. Some studies (Caprio and Summers, 1993; Demirgüç-Kunt and Detragiache, 1998) have shown that the benefits of a liberalized financial system can be offset by negative externalities, including liquidity and banking crises. Moreover, as a wide range of empirical studies on developing capital markets have shown (Agarwal et al., 1999; Baekert and Harvey, 1997; DeSantis and İmrohoroğlu, 1997; Henry, 2000; Kim and Singal, 2000), increased market integration can directly impact market volatility in emerging markets and such financial integration often also correlates with additional contagion effects during a crisis. Nevertheless, these reforms do not often tackle a more serious problem in emerging markets, namely state-owned bank insolvency.

Traditionally, in developed financial markets, bank insolvency is dealt with by using a combination of public or private remedies. Public remedies include the utilization of a legal framework to liquidate a firm's assets. Other private remedies include restructuring a bank's debt in coordination with its conditions. This type of remedy is not generally feasible in most transition economies. On the one hand, these economies tend to have a weak legal infrastructure. In this context, private domestic players are either not present or capable of coordinating bank restructuring because the banking system is dominated by the public sector. Moreover, transition economies tend to have poorly developed debt markets. In turn, the buildup of domestic debt prompts the inability of government to reduce fiscal deficits.

The early warning literature on financial crises (Glick and Hutchinson, 2001; Kaminsky and Reinhart, 1998, 1999; McKinnon and Pill, 1997; Rossi, 1999) have typically pinpointed excessive bank lending as a critical precursor to a currency crisis. This literature is premised on the anticipation that the overly risky lending practices by banks is driven by the expectation of a bailout by the government or by international creditors. The moral hazard hypothesis, as expressed by Akerlof and Romer (1993) and others, is intrinsically linked to growing financial liberalization in transition economies. According to McKinnon and Pill (2001: 326) the resulting financial opening induces a "resulting surge of optimism or euphoria", culminating in a speculative bubble.

These theoretical analyses, though, have tended to ignore a different facet of a moral hazard crisis. The banking system in emerging markets is fraught by financial distress caused by a continuing cycle of mounting bad loans and nonperforming assets in the portfolios of state-owned commercial banks. Subsequent analyses of financial crises in emerging markets (Chinn and

Kletzer, 2001) have begun to perceive the ratio of nonperforming loans as an indicator of a financial crisis.

For instance, Demirgüç-Kunt and Detragiache (1998: 13) have attempted to define financial distress using the following basic criteria:

1 the ratio of nonperforming assets to total assets in the banking system exceeds 10 percent;
2 the cost of the rescue operation is at least 2 percent of GDP;
3 banking sector problems result in a large-scale nationalization of banks; and
4 extensive bank runs take place often in conjunction with emergency measures such as deposit freezes, prolonged bank holidays, or generalized deposit guarantees.

These distortions are often a consequence of distortions occasioned by interventionist policies in the financial system. Using the Demirgüç-Kunt and Detragiache criteria for fiscal distress suggests that India and China have shown evidence of financial distress. The ratio of nonperforming assets to total assets in the banking sector exceeds 30 percent in China and 17 percent in India. The cost of the rescue operations in China and India remains to be fully determined.

In light of the special challenges posed by the banking sector in transition economies, the literature on banking reform has been geared toward a different direction. As discussed in Sáez (2001), the issue of complementarities, timing, and sequence of financial institutions (Choksi and Papageorgiou, 1986; Friedman and Johnson, 1996; Johnston and Sundararajan, 1999; Murrell, 1992) have dominated the literature on financial liberalization. The literature has been split among those who favor rapid and simultaneous liberalization of the current and capital accounts (Little et al., 1970; Michaely, 1986) versus those who favor sequenced financial and capital account liberalization (Edwards, 1984; McKinnon, 1973; Rodrik, 1989). Some advocate the rehabilitation of state-owned commercial banks (Dornbusch and Giavazzi, 1999; Lau, 1999). The advocates for rehabilitation often argue that rapid financial sector reform leads to volatile financial crises (Sundararajan and Baliño, 1991). Others advocate the development of a new or parallel financial sector by allowing new entrants into the economy. Most NIS, particularly Hungary and Poland, have been the leading models of new entry (Claessens, 1998; Lardy, 1998).

The 1997 East Asian financial crisis brought to the fore a new set of problems. First, there has been a continuing economic crisis in Japan, Asia's strongest economy. Recently, a collapse in technology share prices has aggravated the stock market collapse in the early 1990s. A central theme in the effort to overturn Japan's recession has been to rid Japanese banks of outstanding and nonperforming loans. Japanese banks hold an estimated US$620 billion (Y70 trillion) in nonperforming loans. Higher estimates gauge that Japan's nonperforming loans could reach as high as US$1,200 billion (Y150 trillion). Over the last decade Japanese banks have been able to dispose of just Y70 trillion. In contrast the American savings and loan crisis in the 1980s took nearly five years to resolve.

The cost of solving the American savings and loan crisis was about 15 percent of a single year's GDP. Presently the Japanese debt problem is equivalent to between 25 and 30 percent of their GDP. Therefore it is no surprise that a satisfactory reduction in nonperforming loans was one of the leading campaign issues for the reform-minded Japanese Prime Minister, Junichiro Koizumi.

Since the East Asian financial crisis, a new wave of literature has attempted to tackle the experiences of the Southern Cone, Eastern Europe, and ASEAN countries. However, they do not provide a good guidance to low-income countries. Here China and India provide an interesting comparison. First, India and China have macroeconomic features that are akin to those of sub-Saharan Africa and middle-income Latin American and Asian countries. These macroeconomic similarities stem from the importance of the public sector. Second, following the 1997 East Asian financial crisis, countries such as Thailand, Malaysia, and South Korea have attempted to tackle the problem of public sector bank insolvency a posteriori. For instance, Thailand's two largest banks (Krung Thai and Thai Farmers) are still trying to arrange debt restructuring. India and China are attempting to prevent a collapse of its banking system by restructuring its state-owned commercial banking system a priori. As such, the Chinese and Indian cases provide a model as to how policymakers in other developing countries can implement preventive measures designed to avoid financial distress instead of remedial measures to resolve crises once they have taken place.

1.3 Magnitude of Problem of Bad Loans and Nonperforming Assets

The problem of nonperforming assets is one of the most critical features of the banking systems in China and India. India's government defines nonperforming assets as a credit facility in which interest has remained unpaid for a period of four quarters. Indian banking law defines a loan default as one that is unpaid for over two quarters, compared with the international standard of one quarter.

The Chinese government does not have a correspondingly narrow definition of nonperforming assets. The classification of loans is provided by the PBOC's 1995 General Rules on Loans (Trial Implementation). Under Article 35 of the 1995 General Rules, nonperforming or "unhealthy loans" (*buliang daikuan*) are loosely divided into a classificatory system based on repayment status. Nonperforming loans are called "idle" or "doubtful loans" (*daizhi daikuan*) and "dead loans" (*daizhang daikuan*). This ambiguous classificatory scheme has a limited scope. According to Articles 3, 77, and 78, the 1995 General Rules only apply in principle to state policy banks (namely the Import-Export Bank of China and the State Development Bank). As Nick Lardy (1999) reports, the most dramatic growth in this category has occurred in the so-called doubtful loans (*daizhi daikuan*), that is, loans that are overdue for over two years.

The magnitude of the problem in nonperforming assets extends beyond precise legal definitions. Aside from its own commercial duties, China's state-owned banks act as the prime lender to other SOEs. Although SOEs produce only one-third of the country's industrial output, it accounts for nearly 90 percent of loans granted by China's state banks.

Chinese banks have accumulated sizable nonperforming loans made to lossmaking SOEs. The People's Bank of China, PBOC (1999), has estimated that 20 percent of total loans by state-owned commercial banks are nonperforming (*buliang daikuan*). In addition, the PBOC deems that 6 percent of total loans from these banks are irrecoverable. Nevertheless, getting an independent measure of the extent of such nonperforming loans has confounded analysts of China's banking industry. Watanabe (2000: 39) concluded, "there exist a number of valid reasons to support the view that Chinese official estimates understate the true level of NPLs by a wide margin." Nick Lardy (1998) has estimated that bad loans account for nearly 20 percent of the portfolio in Chinese state-owned banks. According to a *Financial Times* estimate (Davies, 1997), nearly 25 percent of China's state-owned banks' loan portfolios are nonperforming assets. A more alarming estimate by Hanes and Lindorff (1998) calculates that nonperforming assets in China's state-owned banks may approach nearly 30 percent of China's GDP. Lu (1996) offered a broader range of the proportion of nonperforming loans to total state commercial banks' assets to be somewhere between 25 and 40 percent. According to the Bank for International Statements (BIS), a nonperforming loan ratio of 5 percent is considered acceptable, while a non performing loan ratio of 10 percent is considered dangerous.

A key difference in the financial performance between Chinese and Indian state-owned banks is the magnitude of their nonperforming assets. India's state-owned banks have loans approximating 30 percent of GDP. These banks hold nonperforming assets approximating $11 billion. In contrast, China's big four banks have total assets of 998 billion dollars (Rmb 8,259 billion). Chinese state-owned banks have nonperforming assets approximating 25 percent of GDP. The nonperforming assets of China's four main state-owned banks were estimated at $146 billion (Rmb 1,200 billion) (Gee and Lau, 1999; Tan, 1999: 9; Zhen, 1999: 15).

The dire reality of China's banking system parallels estimates about Indonesia's banking system prior to the 1997 East Asian financial crisis, where nonperforming loans in 1992–1993 were estimated at 26 percent of total loans (Lindgren et al., 1996). The percentage of nonperforming loans in commercial banks in Malaysia in 1996 peaked at 79.8 of total bank loans. The ratio of nonperforming assets to total lending reached 47 percent in May of 1999 in Thailand. China's problems with nonperforming assets also overshadow other banking crises in the region. For instance, Japan's 17 largest banks (which had been suffering from a lingering crisis) have nonperforming loans amounting to $15 billion.

1.4 Outline of the Book

This book has seven chapters in two parts. The first portion of this book (chapters 1–3) outlines the theoretical literature on the subject of banking reform of state-owned banks. Then, chapters 2 and 3 will provide a brief overview of the key institutional features of China and India's banking systems. I will outline some of the initial reforms proposed and adopted in China and India.

In the second portion of the book (chapters 4–6) I will argue that the initial reforms undertaken so far are insufficient to address the more critical areas facing China and India's banking systems. The book will examine in greater detail how China and India have attempted to improve corporate governance. Once again, timid policy reforms to corporate governance are likely to threaten the stability of China and India's financial markets.

Moreover, in the second portion of the book I will discuss the approaches that China and India have taken to ameliorate the problem of nonperforming loans. I will then show that, based on the preliminary evidence for India and China, allowing new entrants into the banking sector is the more optimal approach to eliminating nonperforming assets. I will argue that policymaker's projected utility gains from reform are likely to supersede the projected efficiency gains from the new entry approach.

As will be discussed in subsequent chapters, the critical problem of non-performing loans do not have a solution in the structural differences between Chinese and Indian banks. In the final portion of the book I will address the issue of central bank independence. I will illustrate the different policy outcomes that have resulted from China and India's differing approaches to central bank autonomy. The divergent policies of the central banks in China and India will create a platform for further research into the banking reforms of these two countries. Finally, chapter 7 concludes by presenting a summary of the findings and draws up some basic policy recommendations.

CHAPTER 2

Banking in China: The Institutional Framework

The state plays an important role in the management of financial services, principally in banking, insurance, and the securities market. In transition economies like China and India, the role of development-oriented banks is more critical. Theoretically, banks can often play an important role in fostering the incentive structures of SOEs by monitoring their practices in line with commercial principles. In practice, though, state banks often serve as a channel for the proliferation of soft budget constraints of other firms.

In this chapter I will first focus on the historical and institutional developments of banking in China. Later, in chapter 3, I will shift my attention to the development of banking institutions in India. Although the development of modern banking institutions coincided with the presence of British colonial power, India and China had divergent roles regarding the presence of foreign banks.

2.1 The Historical Background of Banking in China

Banking in China is reputed to have started as early as the seventh century B.C. There were two types of Chinese banks, Shanxi banks and Shanghai-based money shops. The Shanxi banking system served primarily as financial agents for the central government and was concentrated in the northern and western regions of China. In contrast, Shanghai-based money shops tended to serve private merchants and local governments; they were primarily concentrated along China's southeastern ports.

Modern banking in China developed from the needs of British merchants. British trade in Asia was intertwined with the development of similar banking institutions in China and India. In 1853, the Chartered Bank of India, Australia and China, and the Chartered Mercantile Bank of India, London and China, were established in London. Another British bank operating in China, the Royal Bank of China, was incorporated in Bombay in 1860.

British foreign banks operating in China enjoyed the protection of treaties that effectively insulated them from the jurisdiction of local Chinese laws and taxation. The first domestic bank in China was the Hong Kong and Shanghai Banking Corporation (HSBC). It developed from the remnants of old agency houses. According to Collis's (1965) study of the HSBC, the idea of creating a domestic bank had its impetus in the fears of Chinese merchants based in Hong Kong and Shanghai about speculative plans by joint stock banks operating from Bombay.

The HSBC was in a pivotal position in China's domestic banking system during the latter part of the nineteenth century. Foreign banks operating in China, though, had a virtual monopoly on foreign exchange and foreign trade transactions. According to Wan (1999) and Zhou (2001), some foreign banks, notably the Chartered Bank of India, Australia and China, as well as the Chartered Mercantile Bank of India, London and China, began to issue their own bank notes. However, following the foundation of the Republic of China in 1911, a central bank was officially inaugurated in Shanghai in 1928. The republican government also streamlined the existing banking institutions by formalizing the establishment of other government banks. Although the Bank of Communications (BOCOM) had started operations in 1907, the Republican government authorized it to serve as an agent for the collection of government revenue. The Bank of China (BOC) emerged from the remnants of the Ta Ching Bank. Like BOCOM, the BOC also served as a fiscal agent for the National Treasury. Finally, during the Republican period, the Farmers Bank of China (FBC) was also established.

Each banking institution was established for the purpose of undertaking a specialized role in accordance with government policy. Thus, the BOCOM provided credit to industry and trade, the BOC supported foreign trade by handling foreign exchange transactions, and the FBC provided support to landowners and farmers. Together with the Central Bank of China, these government banks had a sizable control over China's banking system. In 1937, government banks held nearly 50 percent of savings deposits and 40 percent of total paid-up capital in China. In 1939, during the initial stages of the Japanese invasion of China, the Postal Remittances and Savings Bank was set up for the purpose of thrift savings and overseas remittances.

For its part, the position of the Central Bank of China was strengthened following the currency reforms of 1935. Nevertheless, the Central Bank operated within the boundaries established by its private shareholders. In 1937, nearly 60 percent of the Central Bank shares were held by private shareholders.

China's banking institutions suffered a tremendous setback following the Japanese occupation. The exigencies of the war prompted the Chinese government to carry out wartime financial and economic policies in a centralized fashion, outside the purview of private shareholders. The Central Bank, together with the three other principal government banks (BOC, BOCOM, and FBC) formed a joint administrative office, called the Joint Board of Government Banks.

During this critical period in China's contemporary history, the Chinese government centralized the functions of the Central Bank by granting it the exclusive power to issue bank notes. The other government banks limited their operations to those areas not under Japanese control. These banks also undertook greater functional specialization. For instance, the BOC was granted exclusive authority to promote trade and to handle foreign exchange transactions.

One of the critical differences between banking institutions during the Republican period and the Communist period that followed was the role of private banks. Although diminished in their capacity during the latter stages of nationalist Republican rule in China, the presence of private banks in China concluded with the aftermath of the Chinese civil war. A single central bank, the People's Bank of China (PBOC) was established from the remnants of existing banks in Communist-controlled areas.

From 1949 until China's first steps toward economic liberalization in 1978, China's banking system was exclusively dominated by a single central bank: the PBOC. The PBOC served a crucial developmental service. Performing a dual role, as a central and commercial bank, the PBOC collected savings and then redistributed them to SOEs based on planning quotas set by the central government.

In order to reform China's banking system in conjunction with other institutions, the Chinese government began to consider restructuring the PBOC. By 1979, the PBOC was finally detached from the Ministry of Finance. This effort, like other parts of the early reform period, was stalled until 1983. In September 1983, the Chinese government issued a decree that terminated the monopoly of the PBOC.

2.2 Public Sector Banks

China's financial structure is currently divided into five broad categories: state commercial banks, credit cooperatives, policy banks, other nonbanking financial institutions, and the central bank. This chapter will focus on the first four. The organization and macroeconomic role of China's central bank, the PBOC, will be dealt with separately in chapter 6.

As discussed earlier, the PBOC's monopoly over banking activities began to unravel from 1979. In 1983, the commercial banking activities of the PBOC were redirected to a newly created Industrial and Commercial Bank of China (ICBC). In addition, nonbanking financial institutions were also created. International and trust corporations were established and permitted to borrow from abroad. Since 1984, the PBOC has been split into various banking SOEs. They include a restructured PBOC that continued to operate as the central bank, although a restructured wing of the PBOC continued to operate on a commercial basis, under the name of Bank of China (BOC).

In addition to the ICBC, other specialized banks were established, largely following the pattern developed during the Republican era. Thus, specialized banks like the China Construction Bank (CCB) and the Agricultural Bank of China (ABC) provided specialized lending to industry and agriculture respectively.

Despite the formal restructuring of the PBOC, these four specialized banks encompass substantial labor and capital resources. (See table 2.1.)

As table 2.1 shows, the ICBC and the ABC are the two largest banks in terms of the number of employees, but the BOC and the CCB overshadow their competitors in terms of total bank assets. Nevertheless, among

Table 2.1 A comparison of China's four largest state-owned banks

	BOC	*ICBC*	*CCB*	*ABC*
Number of employees	213,767	569,983	356,864	564,731
Total assets	1,837,926	26,339	1,397,536	12,530
Bank liabilities	1,756,644	26,339	1,358,245	12,082
Profit/loss ratio	1.1	1	1.05	1.1
Gross profits (1998) US$ million	$425	$417	$1,215	$95

Source: "The top 1,000 World banks," *The Banker*, 1999.
BOC, People's Bank of China; ICBC, Industrial and Commercial Bank of China; CCB, China Construction Bank; ABC, Agricultural Bank of China.

the so-called big four state-owned commercial banks, the CCB is the most profitable. This suggests that the BOC's position of dominance has been threatened by the remaining state-owned commercial banks.

The gradual erosion of the prominence of the PBOC has had other effects. Qian and Weingast (1996) have argued that one of the principal consequences of the splitting of the PBOC has been the increase in the financial autonomy of provincial and local-level governments and the decentralization of decision-making to households and enterprises. Since 1998, one of the key institutional changes in the PRC has been the restructuring of branch networks of the BOC. Nine regional branches of the BOC replaced the existing 32 provincial branches. The purpose of this policy was to isolate the operations of the PBOC from what the central government deemed to be improper local interference.

In most financial systems, commercial banks are the most important of all types of depository institutions. Banks in China operate under the legal umbrella of four directives initially promulgated by the Third Plenary Session of the Eleventh Chinese Communist Party (CCP) Central Committee in December 1978. In 1995, the State Council approved these four directives. Each of the four statutes touched on a different aspect of China's financial system. One law concerned the operation of the PBOC, another the operation of commercial banks, and the last two include the Law of the People's Republic of China on Negotiable Instruments and the Insurance Law of the People's Republic of China.

Based on these statutes, the 1995 Commercial Banking Law provided the framework for the structure and operation of state-owned commercial banks. As detailed in Article 3 of the 1995 Law, in addition to demand deposit accounts, state commercial banks offer many other forms of deposit accounts, including time and saving accounts. With respect to loans, commercial banks can usually accommodate all types of borrowing and are empowered to make not only commercial loans, but also consumer and mortgage loans. Nevertheless, Article 38 of the 1995 Law provides that commercial banks shall determine the loan interest rate "in accordance with the upper and lower limits for loan interest rates prescribed by the People's Bank of China."

In an effort to transform state commercial banks into independent commercial entities, the 1995 Law of the People's Republic of China on Commercial Banks has tried to promote the operation of a second tier of commercial banks. Competing with the "big four" state-owned commercial banks is a second tier of nineteen smaller state-owned national commercial banks. These joint stock commercial banks include the BOCOM, CITIC

Table 2.2 Comparison of the three principal state-owned nation-wide commercial banks

	BOCOM	*CMB*	*Xiamen International*
No. of branches	97	13	2
Total assets (US$ million)	58,454	16,679	1,208
Gross profits (US$ million)	322	242	22

Source: Ho, 1999.

International Bank, Xiamen Industrial Bank, the China Merchants Bank (CMB), China Everbright Bank, and Hua Xia Bank. (See table 2.2.)

As table 2.2 shows, BOCOM, in the second tier of state-owned banks, has total assets that can rival the *big four* banks. BOCOM and the CITIC International Bank were the first two comprehensive commercial banks in China. Its shareholders include central, regional, and local government agencies. One of the advantages that these banks enjoy is that they are not subject to the restrictive policy-lending requirements of the State Council.

The progress of Xiamen International Bank (China's first foreign joint venture in financial services) is a notable factor since 1985. The advancement of second-tier banks in China's financial landscape gives the impression that the decentralization of financial authority to the regions has had some effects. However, despite the purported decentralization of financial authority, the four main state-owned banks hold over 70 percent of system deposits and account for over 90 percent of banking business in China. Moreover, the consolidated fixed and liquid assets of the second tier of state-owned commercial banks do not surpass those of the smallest of the four state-owned banks.

A third tier of China's commercial banks includes shareholding regional commercial banks. These include the GF Bank, Shanghai Pudong Development Bank, Shenzhen Development Bank, Zhao Shang Bank, and Hai Nan Development Bank. Many of these regional commercial banks are the development banks for the five special economic zones that were established in China during the initial stages of Deng Xiaoping's economic modernization plan. Thus, continuing the trend toward policy experimentation at the local level, the Pudong Development Bank and the Shenzhen Development Bank were the first two banks to be listed in a stock exchange.

China's banking system also includes three policy banks: the State Development Bank, the Export-Import Bank of China, and the Agricultural

Development Bank of China. Since 1994, these policy banks functioned with the purpose of handling policy-related lending related to central government plans. By focusing on directed lending, rather than on commercial business loans, the three policy banks have reduced the policy lending obligations by the four main state commercial banks. Each of these policy banks provides credit for specialized sections of the economy. The State Development Bank grants loans for capital investment projects and physical infrastructure, the Agricultural Development Bank extends credit for comprehensive agricultural development, and the Export-Import Bank provides trade credit, export insurance, and working capital loans to export-oriented technological enterprises.

2.3   *Urban and Regional Credit Cooperatives*

China's banking system also features other types of banking institutions, which are unique to its command economy. These include rural and urban credit cooperatives (RCCs and UCCs respectively). These credit cooperatives are depository institutions established for the primary purpose of encouraging thrift among persons of modest means.

RCCs are small financial cooperatives, collectively owned by farmers through equity stock. RCCs serve as the principal vehicles for holding personal savings in rural areas. RCCs also accept deposits associated with rural enterprises. In the early 1950s, RCCs formed an integral part of rural financing. The Agricultural Bank of China officially supervises the credit planning of RCCs. Likewise, the PBOC oversees the deposits and lending rates of RCCs. However, RCCs have the power to make decisions on individual loans primarily to finance farm projects.

In a manner similar to RCCs, UCCs are vehicles for personal savings in medium- and large-sized cities. Although they are nominally controlled by government agencies, UCCs enjoy a certain degree of autonomy. UCCs emerged for the purpose of filling the gaps in access to PBOC and other specialized bank branches. The first UCC in China was set up in 1979. UCCs collect deposits and grant loans to urban collectively owned enterprises, small-sized SOEs, individuals, and private enterprises at the urban and township level.

Despite the high numbers of RCCs (over 60,000 nationwide), the market share for these institutions are not great. RCCs constitute about 10 percent of total loan-market share. The fate of RCCs may follow the example of transformation in UCCs. Between 1996 and 1998, over 5,000 UCCs were restructured to form 88 city commercial banks as well as 3,240 consolidated

UCCs. Nevertheless, UCCs still account for approximately 3 percent of total loan-market share.

2.4 Domestic Private Banks

The presence of private banks in China is negligible. In October 1986, the PBOC authorized the establishment of the Huitong Cooperative Bank of Chengdu (HCBC). The HCBC was the first nongovernmental joint stock financial firm in China, in effect becoming China's first private banking institution since 1949. The HCBC was set up as an experimental exercise by a group of academics from the Sichuan Academy of Social Sciences. The HCBC has the characteristics of a private bank in so far as the bank's capital is pooled by the public issuance of stocks to individuals. The holders of HCBC stock are paid annual dividends based on the bank's profitability.

Although the HCBC remains a miniscule presence in China's banking system, it has served as a model for the creation of a string of UCCs. According to a study of China's UCCs (Sehrt, 1999a), there are over 100 UCCs in China. These institutions account for over 8 percent of total deposits and 4 percent of total loans. Responding to the dramatic rise in these quasi-private institutions, the PRC has incorporated greater control by local authorities in UCCs.

Another small but noteworthy private financial institution in China is the China Minsheng Banking Corporation. Although it is a minor bank (having only eight branches employing over 2,000 employees), it is the first private financial institution to be listed in a domestic Chinese stock exchange. This significant development became possible when in November 2000 the China Securities Regulatory Commission (CSRC) issued regulations on a bank's listing in connection to new rules for companies making initial public offerings. It thus joins the Pudong Development Bank and the Shenzhen Development Bank as being among the first three banks listed in a stock exchange.

The creation of the China Minsheng in 1996 spells a distinctive, yet underdeveloped, change in commercial banking in China. Over 60 percent of its loans are directed to private sector enterprises. By focusing its lending on China's thriving commercial sector, it has accumulated thus far an unusually low level of nonperforming loans. Moreover, since its listing in a domestic stock exchange in December 2000, the Minsheng Bank has shown spectacular rates of growth, recording nearly a 90 percent increase in profits during the first two quarters of 2001.

Given the success of the China Minsheng Bank, the State Council is also considering the establishment of ten private commercial banks across different provinces of China. Thus far, four provinces (Zhejiang, Liaoning, Jiangsu, and Shanxi) have completed feasibility studies to determine the impact of private banks in their provinces. As will be shown later, this action could constitute a major breakthrough for the development of the private sector economy. Curiously, the discussion about allowing more private domestic banks to operate has taken place within the context of the central government's aim to spur economic growth in China's poorer regions.

2.5 Foreign Banks

The final formal sector in China's banking system are foreign banks. From 1949 to 1980, the Chinese government adopted a stringent policy toward foreign banks. Only four banks (the HSBC, Chartered Bank, Overseas Chinese Bank, and the East Asia Bank) continued to maintain a limited presence in Shanghai.

The growth in the presence of foreign banks has been an unsteady process. Foreign banks operate under a series of rules promulgated by the PBOC. They include regulations relating to deposits and foreign exchange transactions. The PBOC has also issued rules regarding implementation of its regulations. For instance, foreign banks are governed by the Detailed Rules for Implementation of the PRC Regulations (sometimes referred to as the New Rules).

During the initial period of economic reform in China, foreign banks functioned with ambiguous regulations geared toward their operation in special economic zones. The vagaries in the interpretation of the PBOC regulations and rules regarding their implementation have acted as the single most important reason for an erratic foreign banking presence in China. For instance, in 1985, the Administrative Regulations on Foreign Banks and Sino-Foreign Joint Venture Banking in China's Special Economic Zones was promulgated. However, the actual presence of foreign banks did not materialize until 1994, when 18 foreign banks were authorized to operate on a limited basis.

The most prominent of the initial regulations governing the operations of banks was the 1985 Administration of Foreign Banks and Chinese-Foreign Joint Banks in the Special Economic Zones. Another set of notable regulations emerged following the adoption of the Pudong New Zone in Shanghai. Unlike the 1985 SEZ regulations, the 1992 Shanghai Procedures for the Administration of Foreign Financial Institutions and Chinese-Foreign Joint Financial Institutions provided a less restrictive set of procedures regarding licensing and prudential regulations.

Although the 1985 SEZ Regulations were clearly limited to banking operations in SEZs, the 1990 Shanghai Procedures did not have a clearly delimited geographic limitation regarding their applicability. As the Shanghai Procedures were eventually introduced into other cities, foreign banks were subjected to a great deal of local discretion. In order to eliminate local discretion, in 1994 the State Council promulgated the Regulations of the People's Republic of China on the Administration of Foreign Financial Institutions with Foreign Capital.

The 1994 PRC Regulations aimed to provide a coherent, prudential regulatory framework for foreign banks operating in China. The 1994 Regulations defined the incorporation procedures as well as dissolution and liquidation and outlined the scope of business of financial institutions with foreign capital.

However, some of the provisions in the 1994 Regulations did not clarify some basic operational stipulations. For instance, Chapter 1, Article 2 (5) suggests, "the regions where financial institutions with foreign capital are to be incorporated shall be determined by the State Council." An incisive analysis of foreign-bank regulations in China suggests, "a number of provisions [in the 1994 PRC Regulations] are very general, and therefore may, on occasions, appear vague and flexible" (Zhou, 2001: 30). The opacity of the rules has created an asymmetry in information between government regulators and foreign banks wishing to operate in China. Zhou also laments the lack of transparency that guides these regulations. According to Zhou, "in many cases, even foreign banks do not know whether regulations or rules in some areas have been laid down, not to mention the public" (ibid.).

According to Article 17 of the 1994 Regulations, wholly foreign-owned banks and joint venture banks can engage in a wide array of activities, including foreign exchange lending, deposits, and remittances. Subject to approval by the PBOC, Article 19 of the 1994 Regulations claims that such banks may also engage in local currency business and interbank deposits within and outside China. However, despite seemingly ample operational breadth, foreign banks in China are subject to an uncertain approval process by the PBOC.

By 1998, 31 foreign banks were authorized to conduct renminbi business with selected foreign-invested enterprises in Shanghai and Shenzen. A year later foreign banks were also allowed to participate in syndicated loans. By 1999, foreign banks holding a license to undertake renminbi business were also authorized to lend 50 percent of renminbi deposits. Moreover, foreign banks were allowed to borrow long-term renminbi funds from domestic banks. Aside from applicant and location limitations, foreign banks operating in China currently face extraordinary operational restrictions. In theory,

Chinese domestic banks and foreign banks face similar entry requirements. However, the PBOC has decidedly been more restrictive in its licensing approval of foreign banks.

Despite the restrictions, the combined total assets of foreign banks operating in China exceed 34 billion dollars. Among foreign banks, Citibank represents the largest presence. Although its total assets in China are $2.5 billion, its net profits amounted to $2.1 million in the year 2000. The Bank of Tokyo-Mitsubishi has the second largest presence among foreign banks operating in China, with $1.3 billion in assets. Its profits were the highest among all foreign banks with $11.8 million in the same year.

Foreign banks in China currently face extraordinary operational restrictions. In effect, these restrictions have forced foreign banks to provide services only to joint ventures and wholly owned subsidiaries of foreign multinationals. Despite their limited clientele, foreign banks are limited regarding their ability to handle foreign currency transactions from the Mainland. There are nearly 300 foreign banking institutions in China, their presence being limited to maintaining a representative office. Nearly half of all foreign banking institutions in China merely have branch status. For the time being, the presence of foreign banks in China is part of a long-term strategy anticipating further liberalization of financial services.

2.6 Nonbanking Financial Institutions

Another important component of China's financial infrastructure is the presence of nonbanking financial institutions. There are various types of nonbanking financial institutions, ranging from insurance agencies, credit unions, and savings and loan associations to pawnshops. These institutions increase the amount of credit available in the financial system. One of the key differences between banks and nonbanking financial institutions is that banks create demand deposits, while nonbanking financial institutions do not. Similarly, banks may also create monetary liabilities, while nonbanking financial institutions do not.

The most important nonfinancial banking institutions in China are the international trust and investment companies (popularly referred to as "Itics"). They were initially created in 1983. A decade later there were over 1,000 operational Itics. The rapid increase in Itics plummeted at the end of the 1990s. Currently there are only over 200 Itics in China's financial landscape. They vary in terms of ownership type; some are wholly owned, others are joint venture trust and investment companies. Some authors (Tong, 1999; Girardin, 1997) have referred to Itics as a mix of a development bank and a trust company. Itics represent a fraction of China's financial system. Their total assets may not account for more than 3 percent of banking sector assets. However, the importance of Itics exceeds its market share.

Most often, some Itics operate under the supervision of specialized banks or by government at different levels. An Itic serves the function of collecting long-term deposits from specialized banks as well as from SOEs. During the holding period (often exceeding one year), Itics are supposed to utilize the funds to invest in approved capital works projects. At times, though, different tiers of government channel so-called extra-budgetary funds through Itics into unplanned capital construction. Moreover, given its link to specialized banks and SOEs, the politicized direction of the loan portfolio of Itics is fraught by irregularities and mismanagement.

The problems with Itics became apparent in 1998 when three Itics defaulted on international bonds and were forced to file for bankruptcy. The abrupt closure in September 1998 of China's second largest nonbanking financial institution, the Guangdong International Trust and Investment Corporation (GITIC), has sparked a reexamination of the role of these institutions in China's financial sector. GITIC was established as the principal fund-raising vehicle of Guangdong's international investments.

Although regional investment trusts, like GITIC, accounted for a small share of China's banking sector, the repercussions from the banking sector have been large. The significance of the closure of GITIC is that it was one of the few financial institutions that was allowed to borrow from foreign sources in foreign currency. Since then, all the foreign currency activities undertaken by Itics have been terminated.

2.7 *Weaknesses in the Public Sector Banking System and Policy Reforms*

Despite a couple of decades of reform at the margins, China's financial system is ultimately designed to advance the interests of the state. Although there has been a substantial growth in total banking assets (doubling in less than a ten-year period), there has been little variation in the share that the *big four* state-owned commercial banks have with the rest of the public sector banking institutions. (See chart 2.1)

As chart 2.1 shows, the share of the state commercial banks as a proportion of the total banking system has declined slightly from 1990 to 1999. Accordingly, the presence of private banks in the banking system is marginal.

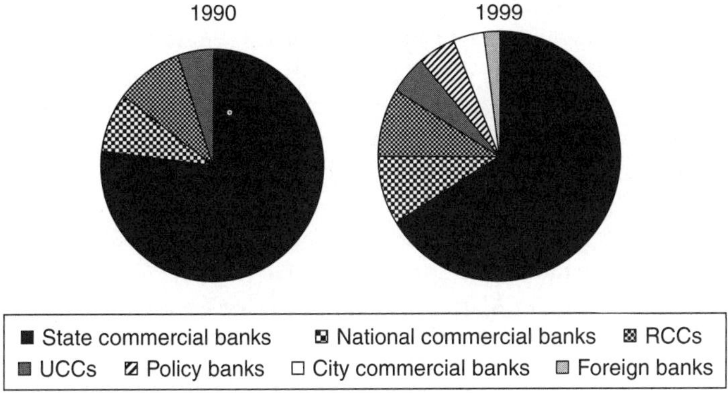

Chart 2.1   Proportion of total banking assets by ownership type.

Source: People's Bank of China, Almanac of China's finance and banking, 2000.

One of the distinctive features of China's banking system is its close connection with SOEs. China's 118,000 SOEs are estimated to employ about two-thirds of China's 170 million urban workforce. Chinese SOEs are often money losing enterprises. Due to their inefficient operation, increasingly SOEs are contributing a smaller share to China's industrial output. According to the China State Statistical Bureau (1997), SOEs contributed about 75 percent of industrial output in 1980, by 1996 it dropped to 28.5 percent of total industrial output. The decline in China's state sector output over the last 20 years differs from the increases in industrial output by collective institutions and the private sector.

The banking sector directly contributes to the inefficient allocation of capital in China. Beijing and local officials channel bank credits to state-owned businesses. Alternatively they finance the PRC's infrastructure projects. According to a current estimate (Tong, 1999) nearly 80 percent of total loans extended by banks went to money losing SOEs. The non-state sector received less than 20 percent of loans by state-owned banks. Hence, Lin (2002) has argued that financial sector weakness and widespread corruption are exogenous to the poor performance of SOEs.

Given the tight connection between the banking sector and SOEs, reforms in the banking sector have been carried out following overall SOE reforms. China has experienced two broad stages of privatization of SOEs. From 1980 until 1993, Law 22.177, gave the executive the authority to proceed with partial or total privatization of public sector enterprises. This initial stage of privatization attempted to increase the autonomy of

SOEs under the contract responsibility system. Under this regime, an extremely limited amount of state asset-management reform took the form of leasing of small SOEs. By 1983, the awards of privatization in China included leasing out about 30 small state commercial enterprises in Shanghai to private parties and transferring 200 units from state to collective ownership. By 1987, over 27,000 SOEs were leased out.

The second stage in China's privatization drive began in 1993. In November 1993, the Third Plenum of the Fourteenth Central Committee of the CCP issued the "Resolution on Several Issues Concerning the Establishment of a Socialist Market Economy," which established a 50-point agenda for bold economic reform. The 1993 resolution included sizable guidelines for SOE reform in a plan that is often referred to as the "10,000-1,000-100-10" plan. Under this experiment, 10,000 large- and medium-sized SOEs were to have their assets evaluated using new valuation techniques. The assets of 1,000 large SOEs were to be placed under the supervision of new asset-management companies. In addition, 100 large- and medium-sized SOEs were to have their control transferred into shareholding companies. Finally, under the "10,000-1,000-100-10" plan, ten municipalities would undergo comprehensive capital optimization reform.

This new pattern of privatization did not take effect until 1998 when Prime Minister Zhu Rongji announced a bold plan to privatize China's SOEs and to utilize $800 billion dollars in privatization proceeds toward physical infrastructure. The Chinese central government has made a binary distinction among SOEs based on size. In a policy often referred to as *juada, fangxiao* (retain the large, release the small), out of China's 118,000 SOEs, the central government will continue to manage about 1,000 large enterprises. These large-scale enterprises are expected to face market discipline by virtue of being listed in a regional stock market. According to Zhu Rongji's plan, the rest of the SOEs are to be allowed to go bankrupt or to fall into private hands. Under this plan public ownership has become increasingly decentralized by the devolution of state control to provincial governments and private investors.

A year after its enactment, China's privatization was stalled by an external shock, namely the 1997 East Asia economic crisis. Moreover, Zhu Rongji faced a variety of internal obstacles to rapid privatization. These hindrances include concerns about widespread corruption and fears of social unrest due to mass layoffs in SOEs. The proposed solutions to these hurdles to privatization came to the fore during the 1999 annual meeting of China's nominal parliament, the National People's Congress. In this meeting, the issues of transparency in governance and labor creation became the central themes.

2.8 The Mobilization of Household Savings

It is estimated that household savings in China comprise nearly 30 percent of its GDP. China has one of the world's largest sources of household domestic savings. At the end of July 2002, household savings deposits reached 8.3 trillion yuan ($1 trillion). Nevertheless, gross domestic savings as a proportion of GDP have declined steadily from 39.4 percent in 1999 to 37.9 percent in 2002.

As is the case in other developing countries, the motivations for saving in rural and urban households are varied. In China, higher-income individuals have a different marginal propensity to save than low-income individuals. In urban areas there are stable income-savings motivated by the expected purchase of consumer durables. In contrast to rural depositors, urban depositors have low per capita savings rate and high per capita consumption rates.

Some economists, notably Woo (2002), have suggested that the higher savings rates stem from consumer optimism about the economy, particularly in response to higher capital requirements. Nevertheless, the Chinese economy is subject to a continuing disequilibrium where state banks are unwilling to lend to small entrepreneurs. Drawing upon extensive fieldwork, Tsai's (2002) study of private venture financing shows that private entrepreneurs rely extensively on a variety of informal financing mechanisms, especially rotating credit associations and ad hoc private banks. Whenever potential asset supply exceeds demand at equilibrium, then credit rationing may have prompted some depositors to save in order to open small businesses. Although there is clear evidence of a liquidity trap, it is unlikely that the majority of depositors have such aspirations.

Instead, higher savings rates may signal pessimism about the economy. Chinese consumers affected by SOE restructuring feel less certain about future income. The gradual transition from state-government income to market determined wages, the emergence of large-scale unemployment, and the sharp reduction of public benefits have all raised income uncertainty. There is significant uncertainty about expected real pension benefits among laid-off or unemployed SOE workers. Moreover, the impact of uncertainty of prospective price reforms is not insignificant.

The employment characteristics of the household also suggest depositor pessimism. There has been a decline in the average household size in urban areas. There is also a decline in the average number as well as the percentage of people employed per household. The situation in rural households is more dire. Although there has been increased marginal propensity to save in the rural sector, most rural households are concerned with meeting bare necessities. The urban/rural divide is affected by income-level disparities. Per capita annual disposable income of urban households has increased dramatically. However, per capita annual net income of rural households has remained constant. Only around 7 percent of rural households have a per capita annual income of 5,000 yuan ($604) or over. The largest proportion (35 percent) has per capita incomes between 1,700 and 3,000 yuan ($205 and 362) per annum. Consequently, the divide between consumer expenditures in urban or rural centers is stark. The lowest-income urban households spend nearly 50 percent of total living expenditures on food (a level comparable to all rural households) compared to 30 percent for highest-income urban households.

The accumulation of excess savings, mostly held in liquid form suggests unrealized purchasing power. In China's case, though, over 71 percent of household deposits are fixed deposits, the rest being current deposits. Chinese depositors are among the most conservative in Asia. The principal reason why Chinese investors have not been drawn to long-term debt instruments is because interest rates are too low and because it is difficult to sell them in the secondary market. What is clear is that Chinese consumers may be reluctant to borrow from financial institutions. One reason for this reluctance may be the absence of transparent credit assessment techniques. As will be discussed in chapter 4, it also points to weak money-market institutions. Retail credit markets are virtually nonexistent. This is coupled with a rudimentary insurance market. Most households face binding borrowing constraints. They rely on personal savings rather than insurance to cover income and other risks.

Banks themselves contribute to the weakness of capital markets. Household savings deposits account for nearly half of total funds for state-owned banks. In contrast, enterprise deposits account for less than one-third of total funds in state-owned banks. Nevertheless, the direction of loans clearly favors SOEs. Nearly 60 percent of total loans by state-owned banks are directed toward SOEs. If measured in terms of loan to output ratio, state-owned banks have a systemic lending bias in favor of SOEs. Although there appears to be some positive development in the creation of a bond market, state-owned commercial banks are reluctant to promote a bond market because it would limit their ability to make loans to SOEs. Likewise, state-owned commercial banks borrow heavily from the central bank, thus creating a triangular relationship between state-owned commercial banks, the SOEs, and the central bank. According to Lo (2001: 22), nearly 30 percent of state-owned commercial banks' liabilities come from central bank borrowing.

2.9 The World Trade Organization and Foreign-Bank Participation

One possible way to strengthen China's banking system is through the increased participation of foreign banks. Based on cross-country studies by Demirgüç-Kunt et al. (1998) and Levine (1999), foreign-bank entry reduces the likelihood of banking crises. Claessens et al. (2001) associated the presence of foreign banks with improvements in banking sector efficiency, including lower overhead expenditures, and interest margins for domestic banks. Moreover, although they find that the net benefits to stability for foreign entry may depend upon the number of entrants, Clark et al. (2001) find that, on average, foreign banks can boost the performance of poor countries' domestic financial services. In the future, China is going to test this conclusion.

After several rounds of multilateral negotiations, China offered to enter the World Trade Organization (WTO) in late 2001. As part of the negotiations, China agreed to review existing laws, regulations, and directives, and to amend them consistent to WTO commitments. In February 2002, the Regulations Governing Financial Institutions in the People's Republic of China were issued. These regulations are the firmest evidence of WTO-compliant policy. The regulations outline a set of targets relating to the types of transactions as well as the geographic location where these transactions would be undertaken.

The clearest expected beneficiary of China's entrance into the WTO would be foreign banks. As part of the negotiations, China has pledged to allow foreign banks to handle all foreign currency transactions for foreign clients upon entering the WTO. The Chinese government has also pledged to allow foreign banks to handle all foreign currency transactions for foreign clients one year after China has joined the WTO. Joint ventures will be allowed, with the possibility of full foreign ownership after five years. Finally, foreign banks will be allowed to take on local currency corporate business in two years, and individual clients after five years.

There appears to be some decisive developments on this front. By March 2002, HSBC, Citibank, and the Bank of East Asia received permission to offer foreign-currency services to citizens in Shanghai. This increase in foreign-bank participation in the commercial banking industry, though, will be initially subject to geographical restrictions, that is, to large urban centers (Shanghai, Beijing, and Guangzhou). It is anticipated, however, that within four years of WTO accession, there will be no client or geographic restrictions for foreign-currency transactions.

Some studies have attempted to examine the likely impact of foreign-bank entry in China. Bonin and Huang (2002a, b) have argued that foreign-bank entry will have a beneficial effect on institution building in China's financial sector. The impact that foreign banks may have in China will depend upon the outcome of recent leadership changes in China. The conservative wing of CCP leadership and many policymakers may fear that foreign-bank entry may provoke a sharp reduction in household savings held by the four largest state-owned banks. When Zhu Rongji became the prime minister of China, he embarked on an ambitious set of capital works projects. These physical infrastructure projects were coupled with an effort to reform SOEs. At the end of Zhu's term, his ambitious projects came to a standstill. To date it is unclear whether they will be revived by his successor, Wen Jiabao. It is no secret that the Chinese government has made extensive usage of bank credits to finance physical infrastructure projects. By allowing foreign banks unfettered access to household savings, the financing of said infrastructure projects could also face some peril. The government could tap into personal savings by issuing bonds. This strategy, though, would be catastrophic if there is a dramatic decline of household savings in China's state-owned commercial banks.

Similar to Wen Jiabao, Jiang Zemin's successor, Hu Jintao, appears to conform to the technocratic, pragmatic mold of the liberal reform wing of the CCP leadership. Having served as the vice-chairman of CCP's central military commission and national central military commission, Hu has built a career in sensitive posts, most notably in Tibet. Given the sensitive nature of SOE reform in China, it is highly likely that either Wen or Hu will probably steer clear of measures that could foment social unrest.

The experience of foreign-bank entry in other emerging markets suggests that foreign banks will have a limited impact on household savings. The example of India, China's most closely related transition model, suggests that foreign banks will concentrate their efforts on capturing the upper socioeconomic tier of urban depositors, small- and medium-sized entrepreneurs, and expatriate communities. Although foreign banks report significantly higher average returns compared to their Chinese counterparts, the profit margins in largely agricultural economies like China will be small. For instance, although Citibank held over $3.5 trillion in assets in India, its yearly profits have averaged out to about $60 million. Even in India's liberalized banking environment, relative to China's, foreign-bank assets only account for 8 percent of total bank assets and around 0.5 percent of all commercial bank branches in India.

As will be discussed in more detail in chapter 5, the prospect for a banking crisis in China remains high. However, the likely consequence of the crisis is domestic. Although Bonin and Huang (2002a,b) persuasively argue that foreign banks will compete for the more profitable corporate and wealthy clientele, the expectation of a general consumer stampede away from China's four big state-owned banks toward foreign banks is highly improbable.

Notwithstanding the unreliable probability that China will abide by its nonbinding timetable, foreign financial institutions, though, will face many challenges in attempting to translate high levels of household savings into financial assets. The most serious, yet the most under analyzed, will be the current legal barriers that Chinese law places on existing domestic banks. In addition to rules issued by the PBOC, Chinese banks operate under the provisions of the 1993 Law Against Unfair Competition, the 1995 Law on Commercial Banks, and the 1998 Securities Law. If read carefully, these laws could undermine any serious effort by foreign banks to make a profit in China, even in the context of a nondiscriminatory environment.

A sampling of these restrictions includes the following:

1 According to Article 2 of the 1993 Law, unfair competition is defined as an act that has the effect of "disturbing the socio-economic order."
2 According to Article 34 of the 1995 Law, commercial banks "shall conduct their business...under the guidance of the industrial policies of the state."
3 The 1998 Law mandates that securities management firms must operate independently of banks, trust companies, and insurance companies. Under the provisions of Article 36, securities companies are barred from engaging in trading that is financed "by funds or securities obtained from their clients."

Overall, even if foreign banks are allowed to compete in a level playing field with domestic banks, they still face operational legal restrictions that will surely hamper their growth.

The *big four* state-owned banks, as well as the second tier of 19 national commercial banks, have invested heavily in bank-branch building. Some of these regional bank-branch buildings stand out incongruously amidst decaying provincial households. Nevertheless this pattern reveals that state-owned banks are prepared to compete with foreign banks at the local level. It is unlikely that foreign banks will engage in high capital costs to penetrate the provincial market.

In principle, foreign banks will be able to provide better and added services. However, the vast majority of Chinese savers will be hard pressed to flock to foreign banks. Although the inefficiency of the *big four* state-owned banks is legendary, they have an added advantage over any foreign competitors, they are free. Low-income consumers are very sensitive to the imposition of bank fees. Efforts by foreign banks to set up fees have already drawn some backlash from depositors.

The threats to the *big four* state-owned banks are multiplicitous, but foreign competition is for the time being one of the least worrisome. The *big four* state-owned banks will face immediate competition from among the second tier of state-owned commercial banks and shareholding regional commercial banks. Among the former, BOCOM, CITIC International, and Xiamen International are the most competitive due to their lack of restrictive policy lending requirements. As discussed here, even if they are allowed to compete with local banks, foreign banks will continue to operate in an environment largely inhospitable to profit making. Foreign-bank competition may spark long-term capital reforms. At this stage, it is unlikely that such an effect will take place.

Based on international experiences in other emerging markets, foreign-bank entry often reduces the likelihood of banking crises ex ante. Moreover, although the net benefits to stability for foreign entry may depend upon the number of entrants, foreign banks can boost the performance of poor countries' domestic financial services. Existing concerns about the devastating effect that foreign banks could have on the *big four* state-owned banks are misguided because banking regulations have restricted foreign-bank expansion. Foreign banks can only expand by a single branch per year and must have at least RMB 600 million ($72 million) in operating capital in order to conduct the range of services and transactions that China's government has promised upon WTO entry. Clearly with only over 150 existing foreign-bank branches operating in China in 2002, these operational restrictions will not constitute a serious challenge to the *big four* state-owned banks, which have over 125,000 bank branches.

With the possible exception of higher-income urban depositors and small and medium entrepreneurs, the effect of foreign banks on the direction of household savings is going to be negligible. In a more liberalized, post-WTO access banking environment, Chinese urban savers are likely to release their disposable income in consumer spending. As such, there are probable expansions in domestic consumption, probably in the form of increases in automobile credit and mortgage lending, which have increased domestic consumption demand. The choices for more prudent rural savers will be far more limited.

2.10 Conclusion

In this chapter I have outlined one of the basic features of China's banking system. The most notable characteristic of China's banking system is the dominant position that four state-owned commercial banks (BOC, ICBC, CCB, and ABC) hold on this sector.

The Chinese banking system also features the seminal role of the private sector. On the one hand, domestic private banks are virtually nonexistent. Foreign banks represent the only truly private sector presence in China's banking system. Nevertheless, as I have shown here, the activities of foreign banks are severely restricted.

The reform of China's banking sector has been limited by the constraints imposed by undertaking optimal SOE reform. Given the tight connection between China's public banking sector and SOEs, reforms in both sectors is moving slowly and on an experimental basis.

As will be discussed in greater detail in subsequent chapters, the construction and subsequent implementation of legislation dealing with the banking or the financial sector is highly centralized. The policy reforms are suggested by China's central bank and the Ministry of Finance and implemented by executive decisions of the State Council or by approval by the Standing Committee of the National People's Congress upon recommendation of the State Council.

CHAPTER 3

Banking in India: The Institutional Framework

In chapter 2 I described the historical and institutional developments of banking in China. In this chapter I will outline some of the key institutional features of India's banking system. Although the focus will be upon modern banking institutions, it is important to recognize that the development of India's modern banking system emerged during the period of British colonization. Building upon the existing network of indigenous banking houses, more formalized banking transactions took place under the direction of British agency houses. These agency houses undertook limited banking activities in conjunction with their trading activities. The primary client of the agency houses were the three presidencies (in Madras, Calcutta, and Bombay), which deposited surplus cash. Eventually the three presidencies established their own banks, the first one being the Government Bank of Bombay in 1720.

India has undergone several dramatic phases in the development of banking institutions. In this chapter I will first highlight some of the key developments in the maturity of banking institutions prior to India's independence from England. The purpose of this historical exercise is to illustrate how colonization embodied some features of India's contemporary banking system and regulatory framework. Later in the chapter I will examine some the critical changes that took place following India's independence until the nationalization of major commercial banks in 1969. The bulk of this chapter, though, will focus on the emergence of new private banks in India since the 1990s.

3.1 The Historical Background of Banking in India

Different types of banking activities have been a feature of India's cultural heritage. For instance, the *Laws of Manu*, one of the most notable Hindu texts (written around the second or third century A.D.) established specific rules regarding moneylending. In the south Indian expanses of his empire, Tipoo Sultan introduced a network of banking houses called *mullicultyal coties*.

During the consolidation of British rule in India, domestic private banks, often with paid up capital, also began to blossom. This period started with the introduction of joint stock companies and the introduction of the concept of limited liability. For instance, in 1881, the Oudh Commercial Bank was founded in Fyzabad. The significance of the opening of the Oudh Commercial Bank was that it was the first branch of limited liability not managed by the British. A few years later, the Punjab National Bank was established in Lahore in 1894. By the end of the nineteenth century, India's banking institutional framework included three presidency banks and 11 joint stock banks, two of which (the Commercial Bank of India and the Delhi and London Bank) were domestic banks with a connection to England. Moreover, India's banking system included six exchange banks. These banks served as the conduits for the financing of foreign trade transactions and facilitating the settlement of debts through foreign exchange business.

One of the central phases of India's pre-Independence banking system was the rapid expansion of the banking system followed by a banking crisis that lasted from 1913 to 1917. Against the background of this economic picture, the importance of developing a domestic banking industry gradually became a centerpiece of India's nationalist movement. For instance, Mahatma Gandhi inaugurated the Union Bank of India.

During the crisis period over 90 banks failed. Later, the Great Depression forced the closing of agency houses. The banking crisis in India opened the door for large British banks to try to obtain control of the existing exchange banks. Another critical development was the amalgamation in 1921 of all three presidency banks into the Imperial Bank of India.

The severe banking crisis led to a reversal in the role that the state played in the regulation of banking institutions. The British established several boards of enquiry in order to study the origins of the banking crisis in India. The most important of these was the Hilton-Young Commission (1926) and the Indian Central Banking Enquiry Committee (1931). The Hilton-Young Commission recommended a unified policy with respect to credit and monetary control.

Prior to the establishment of a central bank in India, currency and credit were controlled by two separate agencies. The Government of India was the sole currency authority, while the Imperial Bank served as the main credit controlling agency. The Hilton-Young Commission first examined and rejected a proposal to make the existing Imperial Bank a central bank. Based on this recommendation, the Legislative Assembly introduced the Reserve Bank of India bill in 1923. The efforts to establish a central bank, though, were delayed by considerable parliamentary controversy regarding the proposed composition of the Board of Directors.

In order to provide currency control and monetary stability in India, the Indian Central Banking Enquiry Committee suggested that an independent institution, separate from the Imperial Bank as well as the Government of India, should discharge the functions appropriate to a central bank. According to the Committee, "the establishment of such a bank would be by mobilization of the banking and currency reserves in India in one had tend to increase the volume of credit available for trade, industry, and agriculture and to mitigate the evils of fluctuating and high changes for the use of such credit caused by seasonal stringency" (Vol. I, Part 1, p. 417).

The period of contraction that followed the virtual banking collapse in the 1910s culminated with the emergence of a central bank as well as the development of a statutory regulatory framework. The Reserve Bank of India (RBI) was created in 1935 for the purpose of functioning as a central bank. India's contemporary banking regulations also trace their legacy to the period of British rule. Prior to India's independence from England, the first banking regulations were enacted. The Indian Companies (Amendment) Act of 1936 included some provisions relating to the functioning of banking companies. In 1946, the Banking Companies (Inspection Ordinance) Act and the Banking Companies (Restriction of Branches) were passed for the purpose of preventing indiscriminate branch expansion of commercial banks.

After India's independence from England, the Banking Companies Act of 1949 (later renamed the Banking Regulation Act) became the regulatory backbone of contemporary banking regulation. The Banking Regulation Act oversees a complex network of banks and nonbanking financial institutions. India's financial system is composed of three elements: banks, term-lending institutions, and nonbanking finance institutions.

3.2 Commercial Banking Institutions

3.2.1 Public Sector Banks

India's commercial banking system is divided into public, private, and foreign banks. Among public sector banks, the bulk of banking business is dominated by the State Bank of India (SBI) and seven associate institutions. The SBI group was formed after the Imperial Bank of India was nationalized in 1955. After India's Independence, the RBI held a majority share in eight banks. Following the enactment of the State Bank of India (Subsidiary Banks) Act of 1959, these eight banks later became the subsidiaries of the SBI. Two of these eight subsidiary banks merged to form the State Bank of Bikaner and Jaipur.

Currently, in addition to the State Bank of India, the seven banks in the state bank group are: the State Bank of Saurashtra (SBS), State Bank of Hyderabad (SBH), State Bank of Bikaner and Jaipur (SBBJ), State Bank of Travancore (SBT), State Bank of Indore (SBIR), State Bank of Mysore (SBM), and the State Bank of Patiala (SBP). The SBI has a controlling interest in the seven associate banks. The SBI is India's largest bank and has the largest international presence among Indian banks. The associate banks of the SBI supplement it at the regional level.

Altogether there are 302 commercial banks in India, with 223 banks in the public sector. Out of these 196 are regional rural banks. Regional rural banks were originally established to provide credit and other facilities to small and agricultural laborers. Regional rural banks were set up jointly by the RBI, state governments, and sponsoring commercial banks with a view to develop the rural economy credit to small farmers, artisans, and other individuals engaged in agriculture.

Since regional rural banks were established for the purpose of supplementing existing institutional arrangements for rural savings, these banks have very limited areas of operation. Their jurisdiction is typically confined to a few administrative districts. In order to develop these institutions of rural credit, beginning in March 1997, regional rural banks were allowed to increase the scope of their lending activities to other sectors. Nonetheless their presence remains limited.

In addition to rural regional banks as well as the SBI and its associates, India's public sector banks include 19 nationalized public commercial banks. During the initial stages of India's independence, private commercial banks continued to operate freely. On the other hand, public sector banking was closely integrated into the development plans of the Government of India.

Since private banks could operate outside the constraints imposed by central planning boards, the Government of India began to remonstrate that private banks were ignoring the agriculture and small industries sectors. In order to correct a perceived imbalance in the lending practices of private banks, Indian prime minister Indira Gandhi issued an ordinance that led to the nationalization of India's major commercial banks in 1969. Upon Indira Gandhi's return to power in 1980, an additional six banks were nationalized.

Table 3.1   Comparison of the State Bank of India with India's four largest nationalized banks (1999)

	State Bank of India	*Punjab National Bank*	*Canara Bank*	*Bank of India*	*Bank of Baroda*
Number of employees	236,000	67,705	55,097	52,571	46,187
Number of branches	8,982	3,822	2,379	2,515	2,573
Total assets	$45.5 billion	$10.1 billion	$10.9 billion	$11.7 billion	$11.6 billion
Bank liabilities	$59.9 billion	$11.5 billion	$16.4 billion	$24.8 billion	$13.1 billion
Profit-loss ratio	14.8		20.9	22.1	49.1
Net profits	$1.8 billion	$127 million	$203 million	$364 million	$458 million

Source: Reserve Bank of India, *Statistical tables relating to banks in India, 1999–2000, 2000a; Rao, Business India, 1999*.

In addition to the SBI group, the 19 nationalized banks form a second tier of public sector banks. Excluding the SBI, the four largest public sector banks include the Canara Bank, the Bank of India, the Bank of Baroda, and the Punjab National Bank.

The 27 public sector banks account for 80 percent of public banking assets and 90 percent of bank branches of all scheduled commercial banks in India. However, the differential between the SBI and other public sector banks is substantial. (See table 3.1.)

As table 3.1 shows, the SBI overshadows the four largest public sector banks both in terms of the number of employees and its total assets and net profits. In 1999, all public sector banks employed 883,189 people and had 45,862 bank branches.

3.2.2   Private Sector Banks

An important distinction between the Chinese and Indian banking system is the role of private banks. Unlike the paucity of private banking institutions in China, India has 34 domestic private banks. As discussed earlier, some of India's most important private banks have a long tradition in that country. Among the 34 private banks in India, 25 were founded before India's independence from England. Many banks founded during colonial rule continue to operate today. For instance, City Union Bank was founded in 1904 and Sangli Bank and Karur Vysya Bank were founded in 1916. These banks are often referred to as old private sector banks. Domestic private sector banks account for 10 percent of total bank assets and 9 percent of branches of commercial banks.

Following India's independence, there were no new private banks chartered in India. This restriction came to an end in 1993 when a new set of small private banks were allowed to operate. Among private banks, most of my emphasis is on the series of banks that were formed since 1993. They include Centurion Bank, Global Trust Bank, Industrial Credit and Investment Corporation of India (ICICI) Bank, IndusInd Bank, and Times Bank. By 2002, the RBI approved two additional private banks to operate.

IndusInd was the first private bank to be established in India since its independence from England. IndusInd has also been a pioneer in internet banking in India. Although having a limited presence in over 30 urban centers, IndusInd has tailored its customer services toward India's expatriate community, or nonresident Indians (NRIs).

Since their inception, new domestic private banks have attempted to maintain lower costs and to produce higher margins through greater reliance on technology. The new domestic private banks are far more technologically equipped than their public sector counterparts. For instance, IndusInd provides very small aperture terminal (VSAT) communications network satellite that allows NRIs to send remittances or to make on-line transactions.

Another advantage that new domestic private banks have over their counterparts is the initial access to equity capital. The new private banks were all established from international financial institutions. For instance, the International Finance Corporation and the Asian Development Bank have equity participation in the Centurion Bank.

New domestic private banks also differ from other commercial banks in its efforts to grow aggressively. Thus, the new generation of private banks has led the way in bank consolidation in India. Beginning in February 2000, Times Bank has merged with the Housing Development Finance Corporation (HDFC). A merger with the Bank of Madura has made ICICI one of the largest private sector banks in India, with combined assets of eight billion dollars. In 1999, ICICI bank had 150,000 workers and 64 bank branches across India. The merger has increased ICICI's customer base to over three million people. Currently, the bank has over 350 branches in 100 metropolitan cities. In 2001, a proposed merger between UTI and Global Trust Bank fell through due to an equity scandal that tarnished Global Trust Bank.

3.2.3 Foreign Banks

As discussed in chapter 2, the presence of private banks in China was largely limited to foreign banks. The role of foreign banks in India is new. Aside from the colonial banks established by the British, the first foreign bank to operate in India was the National Bank of India (later renamed Grindlays Bank). It was established in Calcutta in 1803. In 1969, during a period of bank nationalizations, there were 15 foreign banks operating in India. By 2000, the number of foreign banks operating in India increased to 44. Currently, foreign banks account for 8 percent of total assets and 0.5 percent of all commercial bank branches in India.

Among foreign banks, Citibank represents the largest presence. Although its total assets in India amounted to $358 billion, its gross profit for the year 2000 only amounted to $59.8 million. Nevertheless, Citibank is by far the most profitable foreign bank in India. In contrast, ANZ Grindlays Bank has the second largest presence among foreign banks operating in India, with $287 billion in assets, but it ranks fifth among profitable foreign banks. Standard Chartered Bank, though, with a much smaller presence of $224 billion has produced the second largest profit margin among foreign banks operating in India. In the year 2000, Standard Chartered Bank had a gross profit of $43.7 million.

3.3 Term Lending Institutions

India's public banking sector includes the presence of term lending institutions. Three financial institutions serve as the leading development finance institutions. They are the Industrial Finance Corporation of India (IFCI), Industrial Development Bank of India (IDBI), and the ICICI. An additional organization, the Small Industries Development Bank of India (SIDBI), was later chartered to grant loans and advances to the IFCI or any other State Financial corporation.

Established in 1948, the IFCI became India's first development finance institution. It is a financial institution that engages in medium- and long-term lending particularly geared toward initial project financing and for the expansion of existing projects.

The Industrial Development Bank of India Act of 1964 established IDBI. The main objective of IDBI is to provide financial assistance to large industrial concerns and for the expansion, diversification, and technology upgrade of existing industrial enterprises.

SIDBI performs a similar developmental role. The Small Industries Development Bank of India Act of 1989 established SIDBI. In that role, SIDBI provides financial assistance leading to the promotion, financing, and development of small-scale projects and microenterprises.

SIDBI and IDBI form the backbone of the entire rural credit delivery system. At one level they serve as a direct financing mechanism from both large industrial concerns as well as small industries. At the same time, though, they serve a developmental function by providing support services in the area of technology and management. Operationally, SIDBI also facilitates the flow of financial assistance to small-scale industries and microenterprises by way of various rural credit delivery systems.

3.4   Weaknesses in the Public Banking Sector and Policy Reforms

As chart 3.1 shows, the state bank group and other public sector banks corner over two-thirds of India's total banking income. Currently there are 28 private domestic banks and 39 foreign banks operating in India. Although private banks outnumber public sector banks, they account for less than one-third of total banking assets. Public sector ownership in the banking industry is gradually losing its hold.

The Indian government has been more eager to address the issue of banking reform rather than other public sectors. In November 1991, India's Ministry of Finance commissioned a study of India's financial system. This study came to be known as the First Narasimhan Committee. The report lamented the decline in productivity and efficiency of the state-owned banking sector. The Narasimhan Committee proposed a series of modest measures for operational restructuring. At times its recommendations were vague. For instance, it included the provision that state-owned banks should be "market-driven," but did not specify concretely how this was to be done.

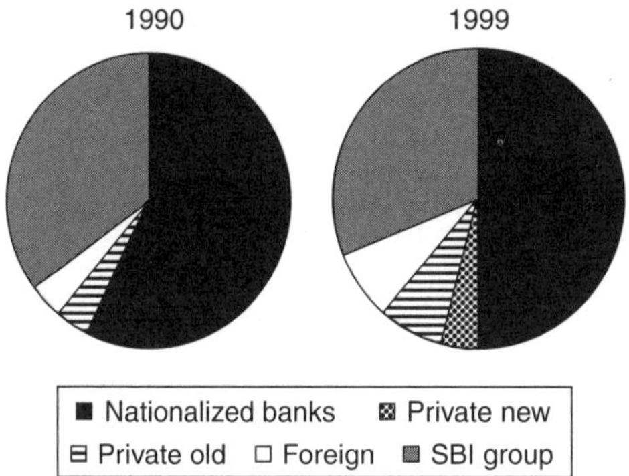

Chart 3.1   Proportion of total banking assets in India by ownership type.

Source: Reserve Bank of India, *Statistical tables relating to banks in India, 1999–2000*, 2000. Figures exclude nonscheduled commercial banks and term lending institutions.

3.5 The Cash Reserve Ratio and Statutory Liquidity Ratio

A reduction of Statutory Liquidity Ratio (SLR) and Cash Reserve Ratio (CRR) are monetary tools often used by central banks to enhance credit expansion. The Narasimhan committee understood that the best way to make state-owned banks more efficient was by enhancing the credit capabilities of state-owned banks. The SLR is a ratio of liquid assets and total assets. It is used to limit the lending capacity of banks. As such it serves to allocate a commercial banks' assets in terms of its choice to lend to the commercial sector or to the public sector. The CRR is an instrument of credit policy whereby scheduled commercial banks are required to maintain a minimum cash balance equal to a given percentage of its liabilities demand.

If viewed historically, SLR and CRR were at their peak in the 1960s. The Narasimhan committee recommended a further reduction. It proposed that state-owned banks reduce their SLR and CRR from the existing high levels of 38.5 and 15 percent respectively. By 1995, the SLR and the CRR had been reduced from 38.5 and 15 percent in 1991 to 25 and 9.5 percent respectively. The CRR was reduced further to 8.5 by December 2000. (See chart 3.2.)

In the 1990s, there has been a steady increase in total bank credit, largely caused by the reduction in CRR and SLR. Although the implementation of policy recommendations is important, it is less clear whether a reduction in SLR and CRR has been dynamic enough to substantially increase the credit/deposit ratio of commercial banks. The credit/deposit ratio is a

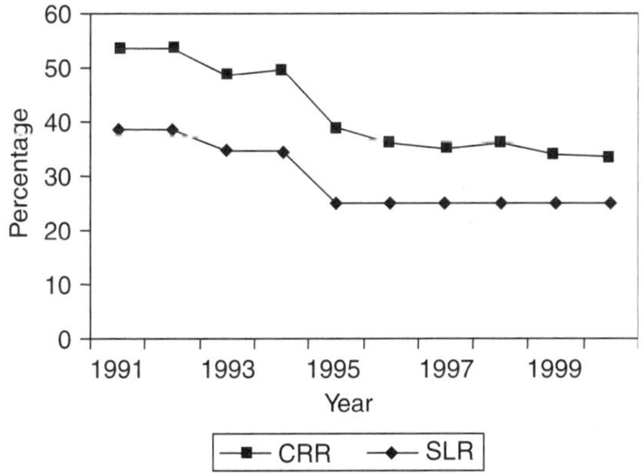

Chart 3.2 Trends in the rates of SLR and CRR (1991–2000).

Source: Reserve Bank of India, *Handbook of statistics on Indian economy*, 2000.

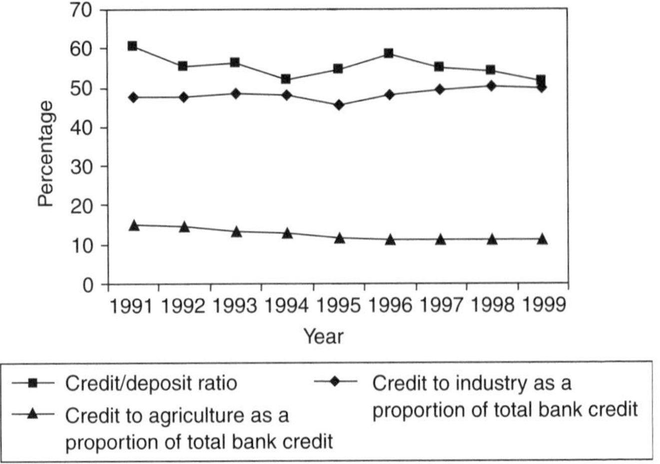

Chart 3.3 Change in the direction of bank credit as a proportion of total bank credit (1991–1999).

Source: CMIE, *Money and banking*, 2000.

measure of total advances as a proportion to total deposits. Hence it is a measure of a bank's aggressiveness to improve income.

Although an improvement over the high level of SLR and CRR in the late 1980s and early 1990s, the current reduced CRR of 8.5 percent is equal to that in effect in August 1983. Similarly, the current 25 percent SLR is no lower than it was in 1964. However, the credit/deposit ratio among all public sector banks has declined.

As chart 3.2 shows, the reduction in SLR and CRR have lowered the credit/deposit ratio of public sector banks. Another effect of the reduction in SLR and CRR was that the proportion of credit to industry as a proportion of total bank credit has overshadowed the proportion of bank credit to agriculture. (See chart 3.3.)

Chart 3.3 shows that the credit/deposit ratio has declined steadily during the 1990s. The table also shows a divergent pattern between credit to industry and credit to agriculture as a proportion of total bank credit. Hence, over the last ten years there appears to be greater private access to credit, signaling a significant effect derived from financial sector reforms.

3.6 Interest Rate Policy

Another important monetary tool concerns the regulation of interest rates. The Narasimhan committee recognized that the success of banking reform was path dependent, that is, it required a proper sequencing of reforms. As such it suggested that the deregulation of interest rates could only take place after a reduction of fiscal deficits.

The Narasimhan committee proposed cautious reforms and warned against a total deregulation of interest rates. The committee relied on experiences from other emerging markets. The Report of the Committee on the Financial System (1991: 43) argued that total deregulation would lead to "excessive bank lending at high nominal rates to borrowers of dubious creditworthiness eventually creating acute problems for the banks as well as borrowers." Although many international institutional investors criticized India's high interest rates, the committee's caution regarding interest rate deregulation was partially vindicated by the East Asian financial crisis.

3.7 *Institutional Restructuring*

Despite its modest scope, the first Narasimhan committee report has proven to be a landmark in banking reform in India, not so much for the degree of its recommendations, but for recognizing that serious problems beset India's banking system. Among the committee's most controversial recommendations were that the institutional transformation of state-owned banks should be brought about by a process of mergers and acquisitions. The committee recommended that India's banking system be divided into four broad sectors. The first sector would include up to four large banks (principally the State Bank of India). These large banks would compete internationally. A second tier of banks included up to ten national banks that would engage in universal banking. The last two tiers proposed by the Narasimhan committee included local banks and rural banks. The local banks would be confined to specific regions, while rural banks would be engaged in financing agriculture and other related industries.

In order to promote competition, the Narasimhan committee suggested that there be no further nationalization of private banks and recommended the abolition of branch licensing. The Narasimhan committee also addressed the internal operation of banks. The Report of the Committee on the Financial System (1991: 43) suggested that the internal operation of banks should be "left to the internal initiative of the management of individual banks."

India's Ministry of Finance released a follow-up study by the Narasimhan committee. The second report, called the Committee on Financial Supervision, proposed appropriate regulatory activities for the RBI. The second Narasinham Committee presented its recommendations in April 1998. In addition to the low productivity of public sector banks, the committee identified the high level of nonperforming assets as the key cause for the low profitability of public sector banks.

The recommendations of both Narasimhan committees have been gradually implemented under the supervision of the RBI. The RBI commissioned a separate independent review of India's banking system. The committee was headed by the chairman of the Industrial Development Bank of India (IDBI), S.H. Khan. This committee submitted the so-called Khan report. The Khan report attempted to harmonize the organizational structure with the lending functions of state-owned commercial banks and development finance institutions.

It is often the case in emerging markets, but particularly true of India, that governments attempt to co-opt a potentially controversial issue by calling for a commission to study a given problem. Many times these types of blue ribbon commissions take years to issue a report. Once the report is released, the once urgent political problem has been replaced by a series of new problems. Alternatively, the recommendations of the blue ribbon commission are discussed but not implemented. Eventually a follow-up commission is established to determine how to implement the recommendations of the previous commission. Surprisingly, the case of India's banking reform led to some reforms. In response to the recommendations of the Narasimhan and Khan reports, several state-owned banks have been partially privatized through various public issues since 1993. (See table 3.2.)

As table 3.2 shows, the central government continues to retain a large percentage holding in equity capital in some of India's largest state-owned

Table 3.2 Comparison of central government holdings by major Indian banks after public issue

Bank name	Date of public issue	Current government percentage holding after public issue (%)
State Bank of India	December 1993	66.34
State Bank of Bikaner	November 1997	75
State Bank of Baroda	December 1996	66.88
State Bank of Travancore	January 1998	76
Bank of India	February 1997	77
Corporation Bank	October 1997	66.33
Oriental Bank	October 1994	66.48
Dena Bank	December 1996	71

Source: Reserve Bank of India, 2000a.

banks. The partial privatization of large state-owned banks is likely to continue. In 1998, the Committee on Banking Sector Reforms (a follow-up to the 1991 Narasimhan Report) recommended that the minimum shareholding by the government or the RBI equity in nationalized banks be brought down to 33 percent of total assets.

In response to the Committee's recommendations, the RBI has established a risk weight of 2.5 percent typically required for investment in government securities to include investments outside the SLR. CRR was reduced from 10 to 9 percent in two installments of half a percentage each.

In order to accelerate the efficiency of state-owned banks, the central government has proposed the increased corporatization of state-owned banks. Among the budget proposals included by the central government in the fiscal budget for the year 2000, the government will reduce its minimum shareholding in state-owned banks to 33 percent. In addition to adopting the recommendations of the Committee on Banking Sector Reforms regarding corporatization, the central government has also proposed that state-owned banks be allowed to raise capital from the market in order to expand their operations.

3.8 Policy Changes Regarding Overstaffing

Other actions to reform the state-owned banking system have been aimed at the overstaffing of the state bank sector. Out of India's 355 million workforce, over 1.9 million work for the public sector. Overall state-owned banks employ over 860,000 people. As shown in table 3.1, nearly a third of India's state banking employees work for the State Bank of India. Although the percentage of overall employees has declined for all public sector banks, the share of employees in the SBI has increased from 23.9 percent in 1993 to 24.7 in 1999.

The seven associate banks of the SBI group also had an increase in the share of employees from 8.3 percent in 1993 to 8.6 in 1999. The overstaffed state-owned banking sector has limited its operational efficiency. Among banks in the SBI Group, the SBI has the second lowest rate of profit per employee ($2,175) in 2000. Among commercial banks, the SBI Commercial and International Bank had a rate of profit per employee of $24,075. Among foreign banks, Credit Agricole Indosuez had a rate of profit per employee of $157,850 (Reserve Bank of India, 2000a; Statistical tables).

Moreover, wage costs in India's state-owned banks inhibit the potential growth of these institutions. According to RBI 1999 Trends and Progress

1998–99, the RBI estimated that wage costs account for over 19 percent of total expenses of public sector banks. Currently wage costs exceed one-fifth of total banking assets.

In February 1999, the Working Group on Restructuring of Weak Public Banks, chaired by V.S. Verma, proposed that in order to improve the operational efficiency of public sector banks, a 30 to 35 percent reduction in staff was needed in the three weakest performing banks. Among public sector banks, there are three whose performance is dismal. These include the United Bank of India, UCO bank, and Indian Bank. The Verma Committee also proposed that poorly performing and overstaffed public sector banks should adopt a voluntary retirement scheme that would affect 25 percent of the staff. This reduction in staff costs would allow these poor performance banks to reach a median level of staff cost and operating income.

The government has attempted to tackle the problem of overstaffing by what may be viewed by Indian civil servants as a radical approach. In 2001, the government implemented the recommendation of the Verma Committee by offering banking sector employees a voluntary retirement scheme, whereby bank workers are allowed to take early retirement. Using the voluntary retirement scheme, the Indian government hopes to shed 90,000 jobs by the end of 2001. The State Bank of India will bear the brunt of the job shedding scheme.

The efforts at improving the operational efficiency of public sector banks ought to be commended, although to date the evolution of this process has not moved satisfactorily. By the end of 2001, the SBI reduced its staff by 18,500 people, from 233,433 employees in 2000 to 214,845 in 2001. By the end of 2001, the SBI still accounted for 24.4 percent of staff in all commercial banks operating in India, an increase from 24.7 percent in 1999 before the reforms were introduced. However, policy measures regarding overstaffing have their limitations. Rajaraman and Vasishtha's econometric study (2002) on the relationship between operational efficiency and nonperforming assets in public sector banks found that even controlling for operating efficiency has not decreased nonperforming assets of some public sector banks (namely the Indian Bank, the United Bank of India, the Punjab and Sind Bank, and the Allahabad Bank). In these extreme cases, Rajaraman and Vasishtha recommend closure with a liquidation of assets.

3.9 Conclusion

In chapter 2 I showed that China's banking system is highly concentrated in the state sector. In this chapter I have shown that the public sector banks continue to enjoy a dominant share in India's banking system. Here I have outlined some basic features of India's banking system, with particular emphasis on the commercial banking sector. An important difference between India and China's banking sector is the degree of concentration, while China's public sector banking is concentrated on the *big four* banks (BOC, ICBC, CCB, and ABC) there is a wider spread of concentration in public sector banking in India.

Another key difference between India and China's banking system is the role that domestic private banks play in the system. As shown in chapter 2, China's private domestic banking sector is severely constrained. In contrast, the domestic private banking sector, particularly the new private sector banking created after 1993, is one of the most rapidly growing sectors of India's economy. Moreover, as will be discussed in subsequent chapters, the encouragement of a private domestic banking sector has been key in alleviating the problem of nonperforming assets in India.

This chapter has also highlighted the approach that the government has taken with respect to basic reform of the public sector banking system. Although India's banking system has been beset by a long-standing array of problems, the Indian government has taken an active role in identifying possible solutions. This process has been undertaken by a slew of government-sponsored fact finding commissions. The recommendations of these commissions have, for the most part, been implemented or are in the process of being implemented.

CHAPTER 4

The Political Economy of Corporate Governance

In chapters 2 and 3, the historical and institutional development of China and India's banking frameworks were discussed. The second part of this book analyzes the interaction between the existing banking institutions and three critical sectors of the financial services industry. In this chapter I will analyze the relationship between the banking system and the development of capital markets in China and India. The focus of this chapter will be on efforts to improve corporate governance, largely with a focus on its role in the development of equity markets.

At first glance, corporate governance issues do not appear to be related to banking reform. However, the special challenges faced by banks in transition economies have led to integrative approaches to the study of banking reform. Similar integrative approaches, such as Pohl and Claessens (1994), have been carried out mostly in reference to Eastern Europe and Russia. Here I will develop this approach further by examining the impact that corporate governance has had on banking reform in India and China. I will show how the Basle Accord's tenets regarding improved management transparency have a direct bearing on the Chinese and Indian efforts to reform their banking systems.

The influence of the Basle Accord is wide ranging. Within the context of this book's examination of banking reform in India and China, the Basle Accord's push toward greater transparency has interesting implications. The experiences of China and India point to several important differences in the source of the push for reform. In this chapter I will show how the push for improved corporate governance is directly linked to efforts to improve banking solvency. As will be shown later in this chapter, the case of India and

China's banks also reveal the difficulties of implementing Basle Accord recommendations in banking systems that rest on an underdeveloped financial framework.

The significance of the discussion about corporate governance and capital market development in this chapter will then be clarified further in chapter 5 as I discuss China and India's efforts to grapple with the issue of nonperforming assets held by state-owned banks. I will suggest that the different outcome relating to the extent of nonperforming assets held by state-owned banks, as well as their likely resolution, exist as a result of the differences in corporate governance structures. Finally, in chapter 6 I will situate my analysis of the resolution of China and India's corporate governance and nonperforming asset problems within the context of the nature of their respective economic systems. I will show that the degree of state interference in economic activity is epitomized by the level of central bank independence.

4.1 *Corporate Governance in Theory*

There are no definitive definitions as to what constitutes good governance. Corporate governance in well-developed markets is a much-studied topic. Shleifer and Vishny (1997) have provided a useful survey of corporate governance. The concept of corporate governance is an elusive term used to refer to the internal operation of corporations. In emerging markets, the issue of corporate governance has been largely neglected due to the preeminent position of the government in industry. In its dual role of manager and regulator state enterprises often fail to protect the interest of potential shareholders.

Microeconomic literature has typically approached the question of corporate governance through the prism of positive agency theory or transaction–cost economics. Those scholars who have resorted to a positive agency theory analysis view corporate governance as an agency problem. Positive agency theory views the firm as an individual agent. For instance Eugene Fama (1980: 298) defined the firm as a "set of contracts among factors or production." As an individual agent, the firm inevitably faces agency costs associated with the dilution of value of a firm. Two leading advocates of positive agency theory, Michael Jensen and William Meckling (1976: 308), defined agency costs as the sum of "(1) the monitoring expenditures by the principal, (2) the bonding expenditures by the agent, and (3) the residual loss."

In contrast, transaction–cost economics tend to view corporate governance by viewing the firm as a set of transactions. The alignment of the transaction with governing structures yields costs. In contrast to positive agency theorists's emphasis on residual costs, transaction-cost economists emphasize ex post facto costs. According to Oliver Williamson (1988: 572), a leading proponent of transaction–cost economics, by "reducing these costs through judicious choice of governance structure (market, hierarchy, or hybrid) rather than merely realigning incentives and pricing them out, is the distinctive TCE (transaction–cost economics) orientation." Similarly, Zingales (1998: 2) defined the corporate governance system as a "complex set of constraints that shape the ex post bargaining over the quasi-rents generated in the course of a relationship."

Other approaches to the study of corporate governance have developed from the principal–agent or the transaction–cost economics perspectives. For instance, Simpson and Gleason (1999) explored the influence of board structure and ownership on the probability of financial distress. In their view, the standard principal–agent formulation should be modified to incorporate institutional features of bank–enterprise relations and the modus operandi of the employees' residual control within the firm.

4.2 Corporate Governance in Practice

Although the theoretical literature on corporate governance has tended to view the firm as an agent, in practice self-enforced industry standards have converged autonomously to give rise to growing international norms. In 1988, the Basle Accord represented the most prominent representation of the convergence of institutional norms. The Basle Accord pushed for greater transparency by financial institutions. Improved management should accompany this greater transparency in the operations of firms.

The experiences of India and China show distinctive patterns of the push for reform. In the case of India, domestic regulatory and industry groups have endorsed corporate governance guidelines in line with the institutional features proposed by the Basle Accord. The most important peculiarity in India has been the development of corporate governance rules developed from within industry groups. For instance, in April 1998, the Confederation of Indian Industry (CII) released the Desirable Corporate Governance Code. The CII is the preeminent trade association in India, often known for the aggressive tone of its reports. The report included detailed suggestions on the desirable composition of the boards of directors, levels of corporate disclosure, and the need for enhanced corporate transparency.

The campaign to push for specific corporate governance guidelines came after a decade of adequate regulatory deliberations. In 1988, the Indian Parliament passed the Securities and Exchange Board of India (SEBI) Act for the purpose of creating a regulatory institution. The significance of this move is that India attempted to establish a regulatory framework before substantial equity market liberalization took place.

The regulatory scope of SEBI was later strengthened in 1992 when it was given statutory powers. Since 1992, SEBI has played a leading role in the development of India's equity market infrastructure. Since 1992, SEBI has been granted most of the powers necessary to ensure investor protection in the primary market. Upon issuance of securities, any company must file a prospectus with SEBI. In turn the issuer of the securities and the merchant banker must comply with SEBI's rigorous disclosure of Investor Protection Guidelines. SEBI also issues regulations for primary and secondary market intermediaries.

Since SEBI's 1992 reconstitution to serve as the sole regulator of the business being undertaken in India's stock exchanges, one of its most critical statutory functions has been to prevent fraudulent and unfair trade practices in the securities market. Up until the creation of SEBI, the legitimacy of certain practices commonly conducted in the securities industry were nebulous. In its role as the sole regulator, SEBI first set out to improve the corporate governance standards of listed companies by conducting audits of stock exchange intermediaries. It then set out to standardize the listing agreement for companies listed in India's stock exchanges. Using this approach, SEBI has been a critical regulatory leader in the development of symmetrical corporate governance standards in India. Moreover, SEBI has issued important regulations for primary and secondary market intermediaries. Following the 1995 Amendment to the SEBI Act of 1992, SEBI was granted enforcement powers to investigate and levy penalties for a wide range of violations, including insider trading and other forms of unfair trading practices.

The development of an increased regulatory role for the SEBI also extended to encompass the demands from within industry to develop clearer guidelines for corporate governance. In June 1999, SEBI established a committee, chaired by Kumar Mangalam Birla, in order to suggest changes to the existing listing agreement. The Birla Committee on Corporate Governance released its report on February 2000. The SEBI (2000) committee viewed as its primary objective "to view corporate governance from the perspective of the investors and the shareholders."

The Birla report closely followed the recommendations made by the CII. Like the CII proposed code, the Birla report highlighted the need to preserve the rights of shareholders and for the equitable treatment of shareholders. The Birla report also promoted greater standards of disclosure and transparency by corporate boards. The Birla report differed from the proposed CII code in that it made more precise provisions applicable to banks and banking institutions. It outlined the stipulations for accounting standards and financial reporting.

The significance of the CII report is that the demands for corporate accountability were initiated by industry, and not by regulators. The efforts to improve corporate governance in India serve as an interesting example to the practice in China. Balancing out improved transparency and capable management has the goal of leading to a reduction of risk within an appropriate regulatory framework. The primitive nature of accounting and auditing systems in China and the shortage of skilled managerial resources enhance the constraints posed by limited financial resources.

In contrast to India, China's push for reform on issues relating to corporate governance has been initiated by the state. The emphasis, then, has been on regulatory forbearance relating to the internal operation of SOEs. Corporate governance in China has taken place in a series of three well-defined periods. During the initial economic reform period (1978–1985), corporate governance in China was explicitly tied to the effort to provide SOE managers an added level of autonomy than that exerted under the *danwei* (work unit) system.

Corporate governance during the second stage of economic reforms (1985–1992) was centered upon the adoption of the contract responsibility system in 1987. The contract responsibility system involved a contract-based performance relationship between the management of the SOE and a supervisory agency. Although the contract responsibility system granted SOE managers greater autonomy, the overall evaluation of its functionality has been negative. For instance, Shirley and Xu (2001) argued that in a majority of SOEs, performance outcomes declined. Pannier (1996) and Tenev et al. (2002) have argued that the failure of the contract responsibility system was due to the absence of penalties for poor performance.

It was not until the adoption in 1988 of the Law of the People's Republic of China on Industrial Enterprises Owned by the Whole People that specific statutory procedures relating to the operation of SOEs was passed. The adoption of the 1988 Regulations, coupled with the 1992 Regulations for Changing Over the Operational Mechanism of Enterprises Owned by the Whole People, precipitated the evolution of a more precise corporate governance regime for large- and medium-sized SOEs. For instance, in 1993, the Third Plenary Session of the Fourteenth Party Congress of the Chinese Communist Party adopted a series of measures relating to the operation of SOEs.

The adoption of the Decisions by the Central Committee of the Chinese Communist Party on Various Issues Concerning the Establishment of a Socialist Market Economic System has served as the backbone of contemporary corporate governance issues in China. The 1993 Decisions introduced the creation of a modern enterprise system and incorporated corporate governance principles based on corporatization. The centrality of corporate governance issues as it pertained to SOE reforms was reaffirmed in 1999 when the Fourth Plenary Session of the CCP's Fifteenth Central Committee adopted further Decisions. Xu and Wang's (1997) study of the relationship between ownership structure and performance appear to confirm the proposition that state ownership has had negative effects on the performance of publicly listed companies.

The performance of township village enterprises (TVEs) over SOEs is well known in the literature on China, Svejnar (1990) found that TVEs had superior total factor productivity growth relative to SOEs. Although the 1993 Decisions formally separated the state's ownership rights over SOEs in relation to that of the SOEs' exercise of property rights, the central factor on corporate governance as it relates to the operation of the banking system is that the state directs credit for state-owned banks to SOEs while simultaneously attempting to provide a semblance of autonomy to SOEs. As discussed in chapter 2, the 1994 establishment of three policy banks was supposed to steer away the policy-based lending responsibilities from the *big four* state-owned banks. Nevertheless, as will be shown later in chapter 5, lending by the three policy banks constitutes a minor fraction of total lending in China. According to Tam (1999) and others, there has also been a steady growth in inter-enterprise borrowing leading to *san jiao zhai* (triangular debt). Moreover, given the current ownership structure of commercial banks in China, there has been little connection between creditor banks and the transformation of corporate governance structure of small- and medium-sized SOEs. Tenev et al. (2002: 55) argue that banks "have not generally been involved in the restructuring of ownership patterns and they have not been able to control the agency costs of equity, as demonstrated by excessive dividend distribution and wage growth."

4.3 *Challenges for Improved Corporate Governance*

The efforts to develop corporate governance guidelines in India are stalled due to the close relationship between the high levels of nonperforming assets held by state-owned banks and SOE restructuring. The RBI has attempted to highlight the need to enhance shareholder value. In a speech, the deputy governor of the RBI, S.P. Talwar, expressed concern that the nonbanking financial institutions had not acted with integrity. Talwar (1999) claimed that the greatest challenge to corporate integrity have arisen "in certain cases in the non-bank financial sector where the directors have defrauded the depositors" (p. 941).

Although the cases of financial sector fraud have received a lot of attention, as I discussed in chapter 1 of this book, the long-term presence of nonperforming assets held by state-owned commercial banks is the greatest threat to China and India's financial systems. The large accumulation of nonperforming assets can have negative effects on the financial intermediation role of banks. Thus, through improved corporate governance, subsequent reform in the financial system includes, but also extends beyond, bank restructuring.

Bank restructuring is one of the methods to improve bank performance, mostly to restore its solvency and to improve its profitability. There are multiple paths by which a bank can improve solvency. A bank can either raise additional capital, it can reduce liabilities, or it can boost the value of assets. Among the policies aimed at reestablishing bank soundness include the reliance on market-based instruments.

The importance of efforts to improve corporate governance results from two key problems. As discussed throughout the book, nonperforming assets pose the principal problem for state-owned commercial banks in China and India. The reason for the extraordinary levels of nonperforming assets stems from the dysfunctional operation of SOEs. As Berghof and Roland (1997) have shown, even in cases where banks have no intrinsic interest in refinancing unprofitable firms, they may still choose to do so with the expectation of a government bailout. In their expectation of government bailouts, public sector banks have in turn contributed to the soft budget constraints of enterprises.

4.4 The Relationship between Corporate Governance and Bank Performance

One of the most obvious objectives of banking reform is to improve the internal operational capabilities of state-owned banks and to enable these banks to operate in a competitive credit environment. Klapper and Love (2002) have shown that better corporate governance is highly correlated with improved market valuation and optimal operating performance by firms, particularly in countries with weak legal systems. In the case of transition economies like India and China, these basic objectives of banking reform are not possible without a corresponding improvement in the performance of SOEs. At a primary level, the push toward enhanced corporate governance guidelines strikes at the heart of this inherent tension in transition economies.

Unfortunately the measurement of good corporate governance in China and India cannot be analyzed using standard tools. For instance, one method of measuring good corporate governance is to study individual firm performance. Another method of assuring adequate corporate governance is to employ stock prices to assess performance potential. A third method is to measure the firm's performance based on its degree of sensitivity to market conditions. Risk measures, such as beta, represent the degree of sensitivity of a firm's stock returns in relation to the returns of the stock market as a whole.

In developing markets, but especially in China and India, these methods present some problems. The first method (individual firm performance) makes it difficult to analyze the performance of SOEs, their performance in a centrally planned economy is a poor guide to measure future performance in a competitive environment. The second method of measuring corporate governance (stock prices) is also subject to complications because firms in underdeveloped equity markets tend to have concentrated ownership structures, often by a state agency. Finally, the third typical method of measuring corporate governance (market sensitivity) fails to be entirely useful in a transition economy because the performance of state-owned firms is largely insensitive to changing market conditions.

4.5   *Bank Restructuring and Equity Market Development*

Faced with the inadequacy of existing methods to measure the improvement in corporate governance, the Chinese government has attempted to reform state-owned industries by exposing them to greater market discipline. China's largest SOEs are beginning to be listed in local stock exchanges. The only Chinese financial institution to expose itself to shareholder scrutiny has been the Shenzhen Development Bank (SDB), which is listed in the Shenzhen Stock Exchange. Given that only two securities exchanges (the Shanghai Stock Exchange and the Shenzhen Stock Exchange) form the nucleus of equity markets in China, the listing of the SDB represents an important statement about the effort to introduce banks to market discipline.

Although the Shanghai Stock Exchange (SHSE) and the Shenzhen Stock Exchange (SSE) are the two dominant institutions in Chinese equity markets, there are 17 regional security-trading centers. A set of computerized trading system networks, the Security Trading Automatic Quotation (STAQs) and the National Electronic Trading Systems (NETS), were established to link ancillary equity market institutions with the rest of the financial markets.

When the SHSE was inaugurated in 1990, only eight stocks were listed. The SSE was inaugurated a year later with only six listings. By the end of

1999, the Shanghai and the Shenzhen Stock Exchanges listed over 949 companies. The dramatic growth in China's stock exchanges has created a plethora of companies wanting to be listed.

The statutory provisions relating to securities regulation are of recent vintage in China. In 1998, the Standing Committee of the 9th National People's Congress adopted the Securities Law of the People's Republic of China. The 1998 Securities Law outlines provisions regarding listing of securities. Under Article 166 of the 1998 Law, it also places the Securities Regulatory Authority under the supervision of the State Council. In order to streamline the process of listing, the CSRC issued a set of guidelines for companies wishing to be listed. The issuer companies have to register with the State Administration for Industry and Commerce. The primary concern of the CSRC was to ensure the financial health of listed companies. For that reason, it required that enterprises listed in any of the exchanges had to be profitable for at least two years prior to application to that body.

A peculiar aspect of China's equity markets is that they are segregated according to investor type. The equity market is characterized by the existence of multiple classes (or share types) that differentiate between national and foreign investors. Unlike equity markets in other developing countries, there are no specialized categories for individual and institutional investors and general and financial issuers. There are two classes of shares traded in the stock exchanges: A and B. Until the end of 2002, A shares were only available to Chinese domestic investors. Only public shares are listed, state-owned shares are unlisted. The value of A shares is denominated in local currency. In contrast, until February 2001, B shares were available only to foreign investors. The value of B shares is denominated in US dollars in the SHSE and in Hong Kong dollars in the SSE. All types represent identical claims to earnings and have the same type of voting rights and obligations to their holders.

There is a third category of shares, H shares, which are issued to companies incorporated in China but listed in Hong Kong. A closely related category is the so-called red chips. These are Hong Kong listed companies that are not incorporated in Mainland China, but whose stakeholders include Chinese state-owned companies. SOEs typically hold a minimum of 35 percent of assets in red chip companies.

Nearly 99 percent of the market capitalization in tradable shares is in A shares. However, due to China's overvalued local currency, the renminbi, B shares were at one point perceived as reflecting their true market value. By the end of 1999, there were 108 B share companies listed in the two principal exchanges (compared to 921 A shares). The combined B share market capitalization is about 30 billion yuan ($3.6 billion) whereas the combined market capitalization for A shares is 26,168 billion yuan ($3,161 billion). Although there are official guidelines regarding the registration of potential buyers in tradable issues, in practice the sharp distinction between A and B shares has not been consistently enforced. Stephen Green (2003) shows that domestic Chinese investors were able to circumvent the securities rules and have been able to purchase B shares. Chinese domestic investors could circumvent ownership restrictions by using foreign investors or firms as fronts, stock parking, or by other such means. As Green (2003) discusses, sometimes investors would use the passports of relatives living in Hong Kong. According to a Deutsche Bank (2000) study, Chinese domestic investors dominate over 70 percent of the B share market.

The intention of the policy to separate A and B shares was to provide domestic companies with access to foreign capital, thus giving local companies a competitive edge over foreign entrants. The leading Chinese domestic companies preferred to be listed in the Hong Kong stock exchange rather than in their domestic exchanges. Previous research on foreign equity investment restrictions (Eun and Janakiramanan, 1986; Stulz, 1981) tends to show that assets open to foreigners command higher prices than those open to domestic investors. However, they are also susceptible to volatility.

Soon after their inception, the Shanghai B share price increased over 50 percent in 1993, but then declined for two consecutive years. The share price of B shares rallied in 1996, jumping 41 percent from its previous year. Following the aftermath of the East Asian financial crisis, though, the market for B shares deflated. In 1997, the B share price change dropped by 17 percent in 1997 and a further 49 percent in 1998. As table 4.1 shows, the performance of B shares has been mixed.

Based on their performance from 1992 to 1999, foreign institutional investors appeared to be disappointed with the poor earnings quality of listed B shares. The growing investor disinterest in B shares is prompted by problems of transparency and substandard disclosure that continue to plague Chinese companies. Hence, foreign institutional investors appeared to be more attracted to H shares.

Nevertheless, the overall performance of the Hang Seng Index was poor from 1999 to 2000. However the performance of A and B shares in both stock exchanges was very impressive. (See table 4.2.) As table 4.2 shows, the overall Hang Seng Index, H Shares, and red chips suffered a decline for 1999 to 2000. The performance of A and B shares in both the Shanghai and Shenzhen Stock Exchanges have been strong.

Table 4.1. Comparative performance of B shares in the Shanghai and the Shenzhen stock exchanges. Yearly average performance, 1992–1999

Year	Shanghai	Shenzhen
1992	78	117
1993	75	121
1994	74	112
1995	55	71
1996	52	85
1997	73	140
1998	41	75
1999	37	75

Source: China Securities and Futures Statistical Yearbook, 2000.

Table 4.2. Trends in the performance of China's equity markets, 1999–2000

	2000	1999	% change
Hang Seng Index	15,096	17,370	−13
H Shares (HSCEI)	374	461	−19
Red Chip (HCCCI)	1,071	1,306	−18
Shanghai A	2,192	1,494	47
Shanghai B	90	38	135
Shenzhen A	683	445	53
Shenzhen B	138	87	59

Source: ISI Emerging Markets database; available at www.securities.com

The revival of the A and B share markets opened the way for an alternative plan to attract portfolio equity investment into the stock market to be considered in China. Under this plan, foreign institutional investors would be gradually allowed to participate in the yuan-denominated A-share market. For this purpose, a qualified foreign institution investor (QFII) program would be developed as a way to partially liberalize capital account transactions. A similar QFII program already exists in Taiwan. This proposal would ultimately eliminate the need for the B share market. The Taiwan model requires foreign banks, brokerage firms, and institutions to apply for licenses.

Upon issuance of a license, these institutions have limited rights to buy and sell equities.

Nevertheless, in February 2001, as part of its plan to facilitate entry into the WTO, the Chinese government allowed an opening of the B share market to local investors. Local investors are allowed to trade B shares provided they utilize foreign currency. The opening up of this sector of the market proved to be successful. Although the price shares of listed companies are limited to 10 percent daily increases, B share prices rose by nearly 20 percent during the first days of trading. During the first few days of trading, over 300,000 new B share trading accounts were set up, exceeding the 280,000 accounts set up over the course of the past decade.

The extent to which Chinese domestic investors attempt to circumvent security regulations border on the absurd. In a report that appeared in the *Financial Times*, Richard McGregor (2001) revealed that Chinese investors travel to Hong Kong posing as tourists, but with the actual purpose of establishing brokerage accounts in Hong Kong. Although illegal, these tours are advertised as "Hong Kong stock market investment groups." According to McGregor, in the May Day holiday of 2001, "as many as 40 tour groups of 20, each carrying around HK$500,000 cash in their bags, went to Hong Kong to open accounts."

As chart 4.1 shows, the B share performance in the Shanghai Stock Exchange skyrocketed in March 2001 to reach an all time high in May 2001. The dramatic increase in the prices of B shares prompted institutional investors to unload their portfolios of these instruments onto unsophisticated individual investors. As chart 4.1 shows, after a 190 percent increase in value from February to June 2001, the share price of B shares collapsed in July and August 2001. The share price of B shares has not fully recovered since then.

In November 2002, Zhou Xiaochuan, the then chairman of the CSRC, announced the formal proposal to open up the A shares market to foreign institutional investors. The government, though, imposed strict entry requirements to potential investors under the QFII scheme. The full extent of the impact of the opening up of B shares to domestic investors and A shares to foreign institutional investors remains to be seen. In the short term, it is likely that B shares will begin to be overvalued and subject to high volatility. The Chinese government's strict entry requirements in its QFII program will deter many potentially interested emerging markets specialist fund. Over time, the attractiveness of B shares will fade as the arbitrary distinction between A and B shares dissolves in the future. However, a full

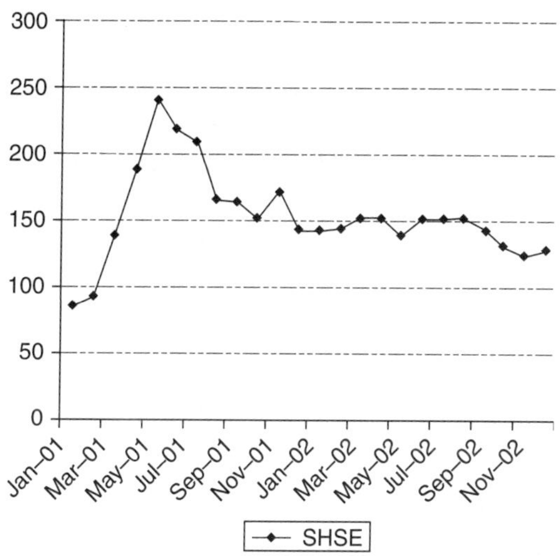

Chart 4.1 B Share performance in the Shanghai Stock Exchange January 2001–November 2002.

Source: Shanghai stock exchange; available at www.sse.com.cn

convergence between these two types of equities will not be undertaken until China opens up its capital account and until the yuan is made a fully convertible currency. Moreover, until the dissolution of the two asset classes, the long-term prospect for B shares is weak because the Chinese government is likely to sell state-owned shares in order to finance social welfare programs. By selling these assets, Chinese stock markets are likely to be glutted with new share issues.

Under the dynamic leadership of Zhou Xiaochuan, the CSRC has been at the forefront of capital market developments. Zhou Xiaochuan's subsequent appointment in 2003 as governor of the PBOC is therefore a welcome development. The CSRC, under Zhou Xiaochuan's tenure, supported bold reforms. For instance, there was a proposal to create a second board in Shenzhen. This new board is to be specifically linked to high-growth companies. The secondary board of the Shenzhen Stock Exchange was initially expected to open in 2001. The proposed secondary board is modeled after the Nasdaq in New York and the Growth Enterprise Board in Hong Kong. This secondary board should provide an important source of financing to the most promising private enterprises. Moreover, the secondary board should allow for an exit mechanism for badly needed venture capital.

The introduction of a secondary board in Shenzhen runs counter to the efforts by Chinese authorities to establish more stringent regulations for disclosure. Small technology firms could benefit from a secondary board because they are not favored in China's current bank-lending environment. However, by virtue of the capital-intensive nature, smaller technology firms are more difficult to regulate. In addition, the opening of a secondary board could also divert investor attraction away from newly listed state-owned companies in the traditional stock exchanges. The fate of these changes, though, will rely heavily on Zhou's replacement to head the CSRC, Shang Fulin. Shang, the former governor of the Agricultural Bank of China, is a far less committed reformer than his predecessor.

One of the most important steps that the *big four* Chinese banks could take is to be listed in the stock market. Stock market listings would force these banks to apply commercial criteria to their lending. Since loans to loss-making SOEs constitutes the most important share of banking business for the state-owned banks, the listing of the *big four* banks could have tremendous repercussions, notably by forcing the laying-off of millions of SOE workers. In the absence of SOE reform, bank restructuring could not function properly.

In comparison to China, India has a more developed securities market. For instance, the Calcutta Stock Exchange is one of the oldest in the world. The centerpiece of India's stock markets is the Bombay Stock Exchange (BSE). The BSE lists over 7,000 securities with a combined market capitalization of US$183 billion. The overall performance of the BSE can be measured with a variety of indexes. The principal index is the Sensitive Index (Sensex). During the last ten years, the Sensex has reached notable peaks (in 1992, 1994, and 2000). In April 1992, the Sensex reached 4,200. A couple of years later, the Sensex climbed to over 4,600 in 1994. The highest value of the Sensex has been in February 2000 when it hit an all time high of 5,933. The current portrait of the Sensex is not flattering. Since its highest recorded value in February, the Sensex has lost nearly 46 percent of its value.

Currently India has 23 stock exchanges and about 7,000 listed companies. The majority of publicly listed companies, though, have been listed exclusively to acquire corporate tax advantages. Hence, in contrast to China, the thrust of policy reform regarding corporate governance has been on minimizing settlement transaction costs and enhancing the frequency of corporate mergers.

The first element in the improvement of corporate governance has been on streamlining settlement practices. The most important development in this respect has been the establishment of the Over the Counter Exchange of India (OTCEI) and the National Stock Exchange (NSE). In order to prevent the risks associated with trading in physical securities, additional capital-market reforms include the dematerialization and electronic book entry of securities. This was largely accomplished by the creation of the National Securities Clearing Corporation. The OTCEI was set up with a computerized on-line screen-based nationwide electronic trading and rolling settlement. Currently all stock exchanges have automated trading of shares.

The growth of the BSE has been blunted by lingering inefficiencies in trading settlement. One of the unique institutional features of stock trading in India is the so-called *badla* trading, namely deferred positions after their settlement. *Badla* trading is a rudimentary hedging mechanism that allows corporations to carry forward their trades from one settlement to another. Trades were settled at the end of each week. Under this system, investors could borrow money from their brokers and postpone settlement of their trades for an additional seven days.

The indigenous peculiarities in settlement practices have permeated the overall lack of transparency in the process of securities trading. Until 2001, settlement systems were paper-based and market intermediaries were largely unregulated. For that reason, since its establishment in 1994, the NSE has rapidly overtaken the BSE as the leading stock market in India.

As presented in Echeverri-Gent et al. (2001), the Ministry of Finance has also been a leading agent for reform of India's capital markets. The Ministry of Finance suggested that additional measures be taken. They include the proposed end of the double taxation on dividends. The third measure is allowing stock buybacks. The importance of stock buybacks is that it facilitates an increase in share price of a security. By November 1998, all three measures have been implemented through legislation.

A second feature relating to improved corporate governance in India has been corporate takeovers. A crucial change took place in February 1997 when the Indian government announced several amendments to the Companies Act. One of the measures allows domestic companies to take over other Indian companies. Under the provisions of the amendments to the Companies Act, a new takeover code was suggested in order to make corporate takeovers more transparent. Another important development in the growth of market capitalization in India has been the access given to foreign institutional investors to Indian capital markets upon registration with SEBI. Moreover, foreign institutional investors are allowed to participate directly in the public offers in takeover and buyback offers of companies.

In addition to enabling greater liberalization of capital markets, SEBI has become the most critical institution in the development and supervision of equity market reforms. One of the drawbacks of SEBI is that its jurisdiction is limited to the supervision of private companies listed in India's stock exchanges. As such, market anomalies in India's dominant state-owned sector bypass SEBI's rigorous demands.

4.6 Problems and Prospects of Corporate Governance Restructuring

The path followed by India and China relating to improved corporate governance has differed according to local needs. In China, the government has attempted to improve corporate governance by exposing firms to market discipline. In India, where capital markets are more developed, the policy thrust has been on refining the regulatory environment, particularly with respect to settlement trading and corporate mergers and acquisitions. These differences in the approaches followed by India and China point to the likely obstacles that both countries will face.

Some of the biggest problems facing corporate governance in China have been its lax accounting standards. Since 1992, one body undertakes the regulation of China's securities markets: the Securities Commission of the State Council (SCSC). The SCSC is a policymaking body that operates under the direct control of the State Council. The commission was a policymaking body composed of the heads of the key ministerial bodies dealing with China's economy. Until its abolition in 1998, the SCSC formulated regulations dealing with the standardization of securities transactions.

The most important component of the SCSC was an executive body called the China Securities Regulatory Commission (CSRC). In an effort to streamline the regulatory institutions, the SCSC was abolished, transferring its regulatory functions to the CSRC. The key task of the CSRC has been to attempt to provide a standardized regulatory framework for publicly listed companies. This was difficult because the Standing Committee of the National People's Congress did not adopt China's first securities law until December 1998. Since 1996, some of the enforcement duties of the CSRC have been delegated to local regulatory agencies. However, the delegation of regulatory authority has come with some costs. The CSRC's securities regulations for publicly listed companies have at times come in conflict with the disclosure requirements of the stock exchanges.

Under the guidance of Laura Cha, the vice chairman of the CSRC, new measures have been proposed to increase the independence of boards of directors and to require listed companies to report on methods that they have employed to improve corporate governance. The urgency of these measures was uncovered when Wang Xuebing, the former governor of the Bank of China, was accused of loan fraud and other irregularities.

A long-term plan also includes the development of an open-ended mutual fund industry. China launched its first closed-end mutual fund in 1998. Currently, the mutual fund industry is regulated by provisional investment rules. China has a thriving business in private mutual funds not officially sanctioned by the state. According to a report undertaken by the director of the nonbanks financial institutions wing of the PBOC, Xia Bing calculates that the underground mutual fund industry exceeds RMB 700 billion ($85 billion), far overshadowing the RMB 85 billion managed by state-owned mutual funds. In light of this evidence, China has declared its intention to allow joint venture fund management companies to engage in fund management on par with officially sanctioned Chinese firms. (Green, 2003)

As the experience of India has shown, however, the prospect for the development of an open mutual fund industry creates its own set of problems. Since 1987, India has a mutual fund industry that includes financial institutions and bank-sponsored mutual funds. The mutual fund industry was opened up to private entities in 1993. Fast growing, privately managed mutual funds account for a third of India's mutual fund market. However, India's mutual fund industry remains heavily dominated by a single state-owned mutual fund group, the Unit Trust of India (UTI). Nearly 60 percent of India's mutual funds market is controlled by this entity.

In July 2001, UTI imposed a six-month freeze on redemptions and sales of its leading fund, US-64. The move was undertaken to prevent a freefall in the share price of US-64 units. In response, the Ministry of Finance sponsored a onetime buyback program aimed to protect small investors. UTI was then forced to repurchase substantial units of this fund at a steep discount. The scandal prompted the firing and subsequent arrest of UTI's chairman, Pavagada Subramanyan.

Bailey and Jagtiani (1994) argue that foreign investors, especially institutions, prefer to invest in larger companies where there is greater financial disclosure and better information. The quandary for investors in companies in Chinese stock exchanges is the rampant falsification of corporate accounts to inflate their shares. The CSRC has attempted to prevent the fraudulent disclosure by listed companies. For instance, the CSRC stopped trading in shares of a biotechnology company called Guangxia Industry for falsifying its reported exports.

The biggest problem for potential investors in Chinese markets is uncovering the peculiarities of Chinese accounting standards. The purpose of the alignment of Chinese accounting standards with international standards was to facilitate the PRC's entry into the WTO. However, one of the unintended consequences of the revision of Chinese accounting standards will be a reevaluation of the earnings of the listed SOEs. According to a study by the Deutsche Bank (Deutsche Bank, 2000), the divergence in the earnings using Chinese accounting versus international accounting standards was dramatic. For instance, the study showed that in 1999 Jinqiao reported earnings of RMB 47 million. If measured using international accounting standards, then Jinqiao showed a loss of RMB 223 million.

China has attempted to come to terms with its imperfect regulatory system by drafting clear rules of corporate governance. In December 1998, the Standing Committee of the National People's Congress adopted the Securities Law of the PRC. Since the Securities Law is the first of its kind in China, it represents a significant step in the improvement of corporate governance of that country. Since taking effect, the Securities Law has taken the form of guidelines issued by the CSRC, under the guidance of the State Council.

The CSRC issued a set of guidelines for listing suspension and termination of listed companies that operated at a loss. In accordance with Article 55(5) of the 1998 Securities Law, a listed company can be suspended if it operates at a loss for two consecutive years. The Chinese government was faced with the implementation of these rules. In April 2001, the CSRC authorized the delisting of a small Shanghai electronics firm called Shanghai Narcissus Electric Appliance Company. This corporation was primarily engaged in the manufacturing of dishwashers and domestic water heaters. Its financial performance was dismal. In 1998, it reported losses of 63 million yuan. A year later, Narcissus reported net losses of 197 million yuan. After four consecutive years of losses, the CSRC decided to terminate the listing of Narcissus in April 2001. Narcissus is the first company whose listing was deleted in the history of the SHSE.

The other consequence of the new listing system is to remove listed companies from the control of regional governments and to minimize the incentives for investors to artificially inflate the share price of faltering companies. Under the old listing system, listed companies were often threatened by the CSRC with delisting. Regional governments preempted such a threat by injecting assets into this type of faltering enterprises. If a faltering listed company did attract the attention of the CSRC, then domestic investors could buy shares of the threatened enterprise with the expectation that the regional government could bail out the enterprise.

Other issues facing Chinese SOEs have been the issue of ownership. The ownership of the shares of SOEs is not differentiated according to the different tiers of government. Accordingly, state shareholders do not usually entrust tangible assets to perform the rights and obligations of the major shareholders. In turn, the interests of minority shareholders are not well protected either. In China, it is not uncommon for senior managers of listed companies to also assume top management positions at the parent companies. The potential for conflicts of interest that may harm minority investors are obvious.

The external control mechanism for listed companies has been weak. The costs of managerial opposition to reform are well founded in the literature on corporate governance. For instance, Jensen and Ruback (1983) argued that the opposition from poor managers to takeover bids decreases the benefits for shareholders. In transition or mixed economies, reform of SOEs faces an additional obstacle. Here there is a rise in what is referred to as insider's control phenomenon, namely the granting of excessive control to corporate managers. The predatory behavior by corporate managers leads to the maximization of personal gain at the expense of the companies' long-term shareholder value.

The consequences of excessive insider control have been partially felt in India. In March 2001, India's stock markets were hit with a price-rigging scandal. The scandal revealed widespread insider trading among leading actors in India's capital markets. One of the individuals indicted for insider trading included the president of the BSE, Anand Rathi. The outbreak of the scandal forced him to resign due to the close links that Rathi's own brokerage house had with leading stockbrokers.

At the center of the scandal, though, was one of Mumbai's most prominent stockbrokers, Ketan Parekh. Parekh allegedly defrauded a medium-sized cooperative bank, the Madhavpura Bank, in order to increase the share prices of a number of technology stocks listed in the Calcutta Stock Exchange. The pattern and manner of Parekh's transactions indicated the cornering of shares, circular trading, parking arrangement, and structured arrangements. The CSE also committed irregularities by not charging proper margins and allowing some members to cross exposure limits in their trading.

Price-rigging scandals that have hit India's stock markets over the last few years have forced SEBI regulators to place limits on the backbone of stock market transactions in India. Until July 2001, nearly 90 percent of trading in India was done through *badla* trades. In order to prevent this type of activity, SEBI has proposed a centralized monitoring system to evaluate the fund flow from the banking sector to the entities operating in the stock market.

SEBI initially proposed a ban on all carry-forward products, thus eliminating deferral products such as the Automated Lending and Borrowing Mechanism (ALBM) on the NSE and the Borrowing and Lending of Securities

System (BLESS) in the BSE. Beginning in March 2001, SEBI regulators enacted a ban on market short sales. In a naked short sale, a broker could sell shares without having actual delivery of these shares in anticipation of a fall in prices. The individual can then buy these shares back at lower prices at a profit. By July 2001, SEBI regulations effectively eliminated *badla* trading by requiring that all trades had to be settled on the day that a trade was made.

This is not the first price-rigging scandal of its kind. At the time of the 2001 scandal, the SEBI was investigating a 1998 price-rigging scandal. As a result of the 1998 price-rigging scandal, SEBI has banned three companies (Sterlite Industries, Videocon, and BPL Communications) from having continued access to capital markets. The action by SEBI is likely to have several important repercussions. First, the aftermath of the 1998 price-rigging scandal is going to affect the speed of India's privatization efforts. Over the last decade, India has been struggling with its efforts to privatize the federal government's 246 state-owned companies. The current minister for disinvestment, Arun Jaitley, has proposed the sale of some of the most prominent SOEs including Indian Airlines, Indian Oil Corporation, and Air India. As argued by Sáez and Yang (2001), the tenuous parliamentary consensus on the gradual deregulation or sale of SOEs appears to be faltering. The evidence for this weakening consensus was reflected in the opposition that arose during the proposed sale of Bharat Aluminium Company (Balco).

The controversy surrounding the proposed sale of Balco has been solidified after SEBI banned Sterlite Industries. The significance of the ban is that Sterlite is the new owner of Balco. Clearly, the link between Sterlite and Balco has attracted a lot of attention because Balco was the first major sale of a state-owned industry.

By banning Sterlite from having access to India's capital markets, opponents of privatization have been emboldened to oppose the sale or partial privatization of other SOEs. As a result of the negative attention that Sterlite has attracted other potential bidders for India's privatized industries could be dissuaded from making bids. For instance, another company banned by SEBI, Videocon, was a primary bidder for the proposed sale of Indian Airlines.

Unlike its actions in 1998, though, SEBI has acted with unusual speed to restore confidence in India's capital markets. The 2001 price-rigging scandal has prompted SEBI to proceed with an investigation of three brokers: First Global, Normal Bang, and Credit Suisse First Boston (CSFB). SEBI has decided that CSFB would be banned from participating in stockholding activities in India pending the outcome of the investigation. The ban of

CSFB from stock broking activities is momentous because it would constitute the first time that a foreign broker has been banned from India's capital markets.

A preliminary report by SEBI suggests that one of the accounts of CSFB was used extensively for transactions in select scrips. These transactions appeared to be linked to irregular trades. Further complicating the picture is the fact that CSFB has been a principal advisor to the third of the companies banned by SEBI's investigation from the 1998 price-rigging scandal. BPL Communications is one of the companies trying to bid for the sale of India's state-owned telecommunications giant, Videsh Sanchar Nigam (VSNL).

The latest scandal reveals two sides of India's efforts to improve corporate governance. On one hand, industry and regulators have attempted to set up an institutional framework consistent with international norms. On the other hand, greater convergence with international corporate governance norms has altered existing corporate practices and magnified the opportunities for new methods of corporate malfeasance. While the adequate regulatory framework adapts to these changes, it is likely that India will continue to experience the type of episodic financial scandals that have plagued its capital markets since 1991.

4.7 Conclusion

In this chapter I have outlined some of the difficulties that face Indian and Chinese capital markets. The focus of this chapter has been on improving the corporate governance of state-owned banks. By forcing state-owned banks to adopt better standards of disclosure and governance, an improvement in the overall quality of capital markets is sought. This chapter has also shown inadequate attention to the improvement of the demand side in capital markets.

Both Chinese and Indian capital markets suffer from underdeveloped investor quality. In the Chinese case, excessive restrictions have fomented excessive speculation by individual investors. In India's case, inadequate regulation appears to have permitted the repeated incidence of fraudulent investment schemes.

Faced with these striking problems, both countries have adopted distinctive regulatory remedies. China has strengthened disclosure requirements. India has attempted to provide a more uniform regulatory structure in a liberalized capital markets landscape.

CHAPTER 5

Repression and Reform of the Financial Systems in India and China

While transition economies aim to introduce market discipline into the operation of the domestic financial system, these countries suffer the residual impact of what the economist János Kornai (1980) labeled soft budget constraints. Soft budget constraints were defined by him as the situation where "the strict relationship between expenditure and earnings has been relaxed, because excess expenditure over earnings will be paid by some other institution, typically the state" (p. 4). Under these conditions, Kornai (1986) later suggested that soft budget constraints had many interrelated consequences on individual firms including weak price responsiveness, low allocative efficiency, and excess demand.

Market discipline and swift information flows between firms and depositors can have a palliative effect on soft budget constraints by serving as a mechanism to curtail excessive leverage. One method by which market discipline can be reinforced is through financial sector reform. Financial sector reform includes interest deregulation, diverted credit, and the availability of money market instruments, a flexible exchange rate regime, competition policy, and capital market liberalization.

Huang and Xu (1999) have posited that overinvestment takes place under the cover provided by soft budget constraints. In this setting, they argued, "the efficacy of investments in highly uncertain investments is low" (p. 204). As such, broad financial sector reforms alone will not be able to solve the more critical problem that threatens the stability of the Chinese and Indian banking systems, namely the problem of nonperforming loans. In chapter 4

I discussed the approaches that the Indian and Chinese states have taken with respect to the improvement of corporate governance. As I showed in chapter 4, market discipline was the initial method used by the Chinese state to improve the corporate governance of SOEs. In the context of India's comparatively more developed capital markets, the emphasis has been on greater transparency in market transactions.

Nevertheless, in order for market discipline to be effective, banks need to provide accurate information about its borrowers' outstanding debts. Moreover, the greater transparency in lending must be accompanied by a credible commitment not to bail out insolvent enterprises. In this chapter I will examine the two basic approaches to banking reform undertaken for the purpose of resolving the issue of nonperforming assets held by state-owned banks. I will then show how China and India have attempted to prevent a systemic bank crisis. In China's case it has used asset management companies to shed itself of outstanding debts. India, however, has tackled the issue of nonperforming loans by allowing new private domestic banks to compete as well as by allowing the partial capitalization of state-owned banks. The outcomes from these two divergent policies will show that new entries appear to have worked more effectively. Moreover, in this chapter I will show how Chinese and Indian banks have attempted to improve state-owned banks's profitability through operational restructuring.

5.1 Basic Approaches to Banking Reform

There are two broad approaches to banking reform. The first method is to allow for the rehabilitation of state-owned banks. The other approach is to allow the entry of new banks. The choice between rehabilitation versus new entry is not entirely arbitrary. Most countries inevitably pursue a mix of these approaches. Centrally planned economies in transition have typically pursued the first approach. Hungary and Poland represent the most clear examples of the rehabilitation approach. On the other hand, Russia, Kazakhstan, and Estonia represent the clearest models of the new entry approach. Based on the experiences in Eastern Europe, the success or failure of each method tends to be mixed.

Apart from the examples of the former centrally planned economies of Central and Eastern Europe, the policy option for rehabilitation or new entry have been undertaken in response to exogenous shocks. Irrespective of the shock, these transition economies have to contend with the prospect of having state-owned banks burdened with nonperforming loans. According to Lou (2001: 48), transition economies can adopt a mix of three basic strategies to deal with a mounting problem of nonperforming loans. These strategies include:

(1) bank closure and liquidation on a large scale;
(2) regulatory forbearance; and
(3) bank restructuring.

Asian economies affected by the East Asian financial crisis have tried to favor the rehabilitation approach. The early reformers included Malaysia and Indonesia. Other East Asian countries directly affected by the crisis, notably Thailand, took longer to address the problems in the banking sector. Nevertheless, the issue of banking sector health figured prominently in the 2001 general election in Thailand. During the initial stages of the campaign, the leader of the Thai Tak Thai party, Thaksin Shinawatra, announced that he planned to nationalize the bad debts of the banking sector. Thaksin later offered to set up an equity fund to arbitrate in debt restructuring and inject funds into companies with good prospects. In response, the leader of the incumbent Democratic party, Deputy Prime Minister K. Supahai, also proposed establishing an asset management company to acquire 10 percent of existing nonperforming loans.

The resounding victory of the pro-business Thai Rak Thai party has ushered in a new era of expansionary fiscal policy. Soon after his election as prime minister, Thaksin Shinawatra directed the setting up of an agency to buy and arrange about US$7 billion in nonperforming loans from private banks and about US$21 billion in bad loans from state-owned banks.

5.2 Bank Rehabilitation, Chinese Style

The experience with ex post debt management strategies has influenced the manner in which China has decided to tackle nonperforming loan management. In the case of China, the primary source of nonperforming loans are large SOEs. According to Lin's (2002) study of Chinese economic growth, the weakness in the financial sector is endogenous to the poor performance of SOEs. The Chinese central government has, in principle, tried to tighten hard budget constraints of loss-making SOEs. Thus, nonperforming loan management cannot be fully understood without reference to overall SOE restructuring. Watanabe (2000) concludes that the "deterioration of loans held by state-owned commercial banks was brought about by the deterioration of the SOE's performance" (p. 23).

Faced with the option of rehabilitating the existing state-owned commercial banks or allowing new entrants into the banking system, the Chinese central government has opted for the rehabilitation approach. The disposal of non-performing loans can be accomplished through two general strategies, either asset disposal or debt restructuring. Typically, the decision between asset disposal or debt restructuring is based on a strategic choice. Asset disposal entails short-term asset management for nonviable loans, whereas debt restructuring focuses on the long-term loan management of viable loans.

As creditors attempt to collect loans, asset disposal often involves liquidation and bankruptcy proceedings against debtor enterprises. For that reason, it is the most popular option for nonperforming loan disposal in transition economies with a substantial state-owned presence. Such a strategy can pose a threat to the security enjoyed by SOE workers. Moreover, China's statutory framework makes it difficult to undertake bankruptcy proceedings.

The other alternative, which aims to maximize the recovery value of nonperforming loans, is debt restructuring. Debt restructuring of viable loans can be accomplished with a debt-for-equity swap or a debt-for-debt swap. Since their utilization in the early 1980s, to tackle the Brazilian debt crisis, debt-for-equity swaps have been principally used to deal with sovereign debt restructuring. According to Islam and Hilton (1993), one of the central objectives of debt-for-equity swaps is the reduction of debt coupled with an effort to capture a part of the discount under which a debtor's debt instruments are traded in the secondary market.

The Chinese government has opted to rehabilitate state-owned banks through debt-for-equity swaps. Blackwell and Nocera (1988) also found that, from the perspective of banks, debt-for-equity swaps provide an opportunity for diversifying their credit exposure. Watanabe (2000) argues that preventative measures, such as debt-for-equity swaps, can improve the asset quality of banks and enhance their risk bearing ability. Under this process, an asset management company is set up to buy a bank's nonperforming loans at a discount. The asset management company then issues debt in the form of bonds.

The initial experience with debt-for-equity swaps was not a success. In 1998, the Ministry of Finance tried to recapitalize the big four state-owned commercial banks by issuing special bonds worth RMB 270 billion ($34 billion). The special bonds failed to recapitalize the big four banks. In 2000, the Ministry of Finance tried to transfer RMB 1,400 billion ($175 billion) to four asset management companies.

The most notable effort in this regard has been to reduce nonperforming loans from one of China's largest banks. In April 1999, the Ministry of

Finance set up Xinda Asset Management Company (XAMCO) to help CCB dispose of bad loans. XAMCO's main plan is to raise additional funds to buy the CCB's nonperforming loans in exchange for stakes in debtor ventures, primarily China's large SOEs. The Ministry of Finance allocated $1.2 billion in seed money, expecting that in due course it will buy $36 billion in defaulted or other nonperforming loans from CCB.

XAMCO is loosely modeled after the Resolution Trust Corporation (RTC), the independent agency established in the United States after the savings and loan debacle in the 1980s. Three other asset management companies (Huarong, Changcheng (Great Wall), and Dongfang (Orient)) will aim to restructure the Industrial and Commercial Bank of China, the Agricultural Bank of China, and the BOC respectively. These three asset management companies have been set up to rehabilitate the BOC through bonds backed by the Ministry of Finance.

In November 2000, the State Council provided more precise rules governing the AMCs when it released the Regulations on Financial Assets Management Companies. The State Council's ordinance warned that those AMCs that have entered into debt–equity swap agreements with restructuring firms must act in the best interest of the shareholders. In order to preserve the shareholders' interests, Article 11 of the 2000 Regulations provide that restructuring firms need to obtain an approval from the State Council prior to agreeing to adopt the debt–equity plan. The 2000 Regulations also provided AMCs with an unorthodox approach to improve the corporate governance of firms. Under Article 25 of the 2000 Regulations, AMCs were held responsible for formulating "the operation policy and corresponding measures to improve internal governance structure and set up an internal restraint mechanism and an internal incentive mechanism."

At the same time, AMCs have been ordered to finalize their agreements with restructuring firms as soon as possible. Moreover, the attempts to formalize the accounting standards of state-owned firms have been especially mandated for AMCs as well. According to the CSRC's guidelines regarding AMCs, restructured enterprises should adopt stringent budget control in order to ensure the maximum efficacy in the use of funds. Restructured companies are directed to set up systematic accounting and financial control systems. In addition to internal auditing, restructured companies are subject to annual audits by accounting firms authorized by the Ministry of Finance.

One of the key differences between the RTC and the asset management companies being established in China is that the RTC operated as an independent agency from the U.S. Treasury Department. Another key difference is that the lending parameters of Chinese banks differ from those of

American savings and loan institutions. Imprudent lending parameters of savings and loan institutions were mitigated by regulatory oversight. Instead, Chinese banks have a perverse incentive to make bad loans because they are politically motivated.

Lardy (1998) estimated that nearly half of all specialized bank loans made in 1991 were policy loans. In order to alleviate the burden that policy loans placed on the specialized banks, three additional policy banks (the State Development Bank of China, the Agricultural Development Bank of China, and the Export–Import Bank) were established in 1994. Nevertheless, Park and Sehrt (2001) report that the specialized banks continue to manage the bulk of total loans made by Chinese financial institutions, whereas the policy banks only handle 16 percent of total loans.

Policy imperatives, rather than commercial considerations, is also a determining factor in lending decisions at lower-level financial institutions. For instance, one study of China's UCCs (Sehrt, 1999a) reports that 90 percent of loans are made in response to pressure from various government agencies. Subsequent studies by Sehrt (1999b) and Park and Sehrt (2001) find that interprovincial financial intermediation is heavily influenced by policy variables and not by economic considerations.

Finally, the newly created Chinese asset management companies differ from the American model in that the former do not have the independent authority to fire poorly performing management teams. This authority lies with the ministry that oversees the largest Chinese SOEs, the State Economic and Trade Commission (SETC). Moreover, the cost of liquidating assets also extends to the fate of the employees in restructured enterprises. In the American S&L model, forced liquidation was accomplished through a court order for corporate bankruptcy. The prospects for obtaining and enforcing such an order in China are dim, particularly if the local employees in the restructured enterprises do not benefit directly from the sale of assets.

One of the principal problems in analyzing the development of China's banking crisis has been its government's reluctance to release credible estimates on the percentage of nonperforming assets of its chief state-run banks. For instance, as indicated in table 2.1, none of China's four major banks show a loss. The reason for this discrepancy is that the definition of nonperforming loans utilized in China differs from international accounting standards. Standard assets, substandard assets, doubtful assets, and loss broadly categorize the standard classification of loan assets. In China, only unrecoverable loans (doubtful loans and losses) are considered as being nonperforming after a year of nonpayment. International accounting standards normally consider a loan to be nonperforming after loan payments are overdue for over three months.

The difference in the timing of the declaration of a loan as nonperforming is important because of the resulting differences in interest income that is derived from them. Chinese banks tends to overstate their profitability because interest income is accrued for loans up to one year, the lost interest income before a loan is declared nonperforming is credited on the balance sheets of banks. According to international accounting standards, interest income is suspended for all substandard loans. If Chinese banks used the narrower international accounting standards of three months, then the period of interest income accrued would be shortened considerably.

In addition to the unique accounting standards used by Chinese banks, an added concern with the problem of nonperforming loans in China is that the Chinese government typically minimizes even the well-publicized problems with CCB's loan portfolio. According to conservative independent estimates, CCB's defaulted and nonperforming loans account for nearly a quarter of its total loan portfolio. However, according to China's central bank governor, Dai Xianglong, CCB's nonperforming assets account for less than 10 percent of its loan portfolio (Tow, 1999). However, a recent report by China's credit office revealed that the ICBC and the CCB had overstated their assets by $48 billion (RMB 400 billion).

There have been some recent efforts by the Chinese government to fully come to terms with the true extent of the nonperforming loan problem in China's state-owned banks. Using international accounting standards, the governor of the BOC, Liu Ming Kang, announced that the bank readjusted its nonperforming loans from 11 to 28.5 percent. Despite the initiative taken by the BOC, the other three dominant state commercial banks have yet to follow through. Nevertheless, some Chinese government official estimates for the nonperforming loan ratio of China's banks oscillates from 20 to 25 percent.

Moreover, the 1999 bilateral trade talks between the United States and China resulted in a number of pledges from the Chinese government after accession to the WTO. The bulk of the pledged reforms in the banking sector aim to facilitate transactions of foreign banks operating in China. In the banking sector, the Chinese government pledged to allow all foreign banks to conduct renminbi business with Chinese enterprises. Moreover, all foreign banks can conduct renminbi business with retailers and individuals.

5.3 New Entry, Indian Style

While the Chinese strategy for dealing with nonperforming loans has been a mixed rehabilitation approach, using bank restructuring and regulatory forbearance as its centerpiece. India has tended to deal with the nonperforming loan problem through bank restructuring and new entry.

India's major state-owned commercial banks have had a steady stream of nonperforming assets. According to the RBI (Reserve Bank of India, 2000a; *Statistical tables, 1999–2000*), in 1993, 7.4 percent of loan assets by public sector banks were considered substandard. In addition, 11.9 percent of loan assets were classified as doubtful and 2.3 percent as loss assets. In India, nonperforming assets are subdivided into two broad categories: gross nonperforming assets and net nonperforming assets. Gross nonperforming assets are loan advances deemed to be irrecoverable. However, due to the regulatory time lag in the recovery process and the statutory safeguards available to prevent prompt write-offs, they are in the book balances of banks. Net nonperforming assets are provision-adjusted nonperforming assets.

By 1999, the ratio of standard assets to net nonperforming assets had improved slightly. In 1999, 4.9 percent of assets were substandard, 9 percent were doubtful, and 2 percent were loss assets. In order to alleviate the burden of nonperforming assets on the accounting books of banks, the RBI has announced what it terms a one-time settlement scheme (OTS) for nonperforming assets. Under this plan, announced in 2001, a bank holding nonperforming assets would be granted no dues certificates. These certificates would enable companies to receive a substantial portion of outstanding interest written off by one bank.

Using several performance indicators as a percentage of total assets, Ram Mohan (2002) has also shown that since the deregulation of India's banks, public sector banks have improved their performance in absolute as well as in relative terms. At this stage, though, it appears that the gradual corporatization of select state-owned banks has not significantly reduced net nonperforming assets as a percentage of net advances. (See table 5.1.)

As table 5.1 shows, out of the eight partially privatized banks mentioned in table 3.2 only two (State Bank of India and the Bank of India) appear to have had a decline in the ratio between net nonperforming assets and total advances. However, seven out of the nine banks mentioned in table 5.1 have had an increase in capital adequacy ratio.

In his perceptive critique of India's banking reform efforts, Raje (2000) argued that the early reform period of banking reform missed the opportunity for enhancing the operational efficiency of public sector banks. Raje faults India's banking reform process for its incremental and disjointed pace. According to Raje, one of the mistakes by policymakers was "in considering restructuring issues to be a subset of regulatory reform." He added that this premise "corresponds to the assumption that coping with regulatory best practices alone could ensure the health and stability of banks" (Raje, 2000: 6).

Table 5.1 Ratio of net nonperforming assets (NPA) as percentage of net advances for selected years (capital adequacy ratio (CAR) in parentheses)

Bank name	Net NPA ratio (CAR) 1997	Net NPA ratio (CAR) 1998	Net NPA ratio (CAR) 1999	Net NPA ratio (CAR) 2000
State Bank of India	7.3 (12.1)	6.1 (14.5)	7.1 (12.5)	6.4 (11.4)
State Bank of Bikaner	7.9 (8.8)	7.1 (10.6)	10.4 (12.2)	10.4 (12.3)
State Bank of Baroda	7.5 (11.8)	6.6 (12.1)	7.7 (13.3)	5.9 (12.1)
State Bank Travancore	8.8 (8.1)	12.2 (11.4)	10.5 (10.2)	8.5 (11.1)
Bank of India	6.9 (10.2)	7.3 (9.1)	7.2 (10.5)	7.5 (10.5)
Corporation Bank	3.6 (11.3)	2.9 (16.9)	1.9 (13.2)	1.9 (12.8)
Oriental Bank	5.6 (17.6)	4.5 (15.2)	4.5 (14.1)	3.8 (12.7)
Dena Bank	9.3 (10.8)	8.2 (11.8)	7.6 (11.1)	13.4 (11.6)

Source: Reserve Bank of India, 2000a (*Statistical tables, 1999–2000*).

Raje also argues that Indian policy makers failed to respond adequately to the crisis posed by nonperforming assets. According to Raje, "(i)nstead of addressing systemic issued, the bad loan and strained capital problem was treated as strictly endogenous, the outcome of regulatory changes" (Raje, 2000: 9). Raje point to India's policy makers' decision to recapitalize rather than to restructure as an indicator of the low priority that they gave to the nonperforming asset problem.

Although I agree with Raje's assessment of the critical problem of nonperforming assets in public sector banks, I disagree with his assessment of the need to use restructuring as the optimal instrument for resolving the issue. Although the official inquiries have stressed the need for the rehabilitation of state-owned commercial banks, the Indian government has been more receptive than their Chinese counterparts in allowing new entrants into the banking system. The deregulation and gradual privatization of the banking sector is beginning to bear some modest, yet favorable outcomes. For instance, there is a notable growth of small regional banks. Since 1994, there have been nine new entrants to India's banking system. One such example is the Bank of Punjab, Ltd. The Bank of Punjab began operating in 1995. Since its inception, it has a remarkably low rate of gross nonperforming assets as a proportion of total assets (less than 0.6 percent). Currently it has over

Table 5.2 Net NPA as a percentage of net advances (CAR in parentheses)

Bank name	Net NPA ratio (CAR) 1997	Net NPA ratio (CAR) 1998	Net NPA ratio (CAR) 1999	Net NPA ratio (CAR) 2000
ICICI Bank	1.7 (13.1)	1.1 (13.5)	2.8 (11.1)	1.5 (19.6)
Global Trust Bank	4.5 (10.1)	2.9 (10.3)	2.1 (11.9)	0.8 (13.7)
IndusInd Bank	2.1 (12.9)	3.9 (17.9)	7.2 (15.1)	5.9 (13.2)
Times Bank	0.5 (15.4)	1.4 (11.3)	8.3 (9.9)	***
Centurion Bank	0.1 (27.1)	0.2 (20.1)	3.7 (8.4)	2.7 (15.6)

Source: Reserve Bank of India, 2000a; *Statistical tables relating to Banks in India.*

200,000 customers and over 40 branches. By providing a variety of specialized services to the often-neglected nonresident Indian community, the Bank of Punjab has a larger ratio of gross profits as a proportion of total assets than most state-owned banks.

With the exception of Times Bank, which merged with HDFC Bank in 2000, the performance of private banks formed since 1994 has been excellent (see table 5.2.).

As table 5.2 shows, there has been a declining trend in the ratio of nonperforming assets as a proportion of net advances among most of the private domestic banks formed since 1994. The ratio of net nonperforming assets as a proportion of net advances peaked in 1999 for two banks (IndusInd and Centurion). Their performance since shows a decline. Similarly the capital adequacy ratio of new private domestic banks compares very favorably with the performance of state-owned commercial banks.

New entrants to India's banking system show that nonperforming assets need not be a permanent feature of the operation of commercial banks in developing countries. Despite its wider loan base, few entrants to India's banking system have tighter credit requirements. Various econometric studies (Ajit and Bangar, 1998; Rajaraman et al., 1999; Rajaraman and Vasishtha, 2002) have shown that private sector banks have a higher volatility ratio and capital adequacy ratios and lower nonperforming assets than public sector banks. In a multi-country analysis of various facets of the banking industry, Barth et al. (2001) have found that government ownership is negatively correlated with bank performance. They argue that by not restricting banking activity, private monitoring induces a diversification of income streams and loan portfolios.

Unlike controversies surrounding the privatization of other sectors of the economy, banking reform, and privatization have been controversy free.

Armijo and Jha (1997) speculated that the absence of controversy is due to the expected distribution of costs and benefits between the central government and the states. While I generally agree with this explanation, I would also add that the institutional legacy of private banks in India (some dating to the earliest days of British colonialism) has minimized fears about further private participation in banking. Moreover, unlike the experience in other sectors of the economy, privatization of India's banks has been accompanied by deregulation.

A government's choice between rehabilitation and new entry could be explained in terms of the size of the nonpublic sector in a given economy. In this sense, economies with a large private sector would be expected to be inclined toward new entry whereas those transition economies where the public sector dominates would be expected to opt for rehabilitation. A cursory examination of recent cases would show that the ratio of the private sector in relation to the public sector does not necessarily lead to one outcome over the other. For instance, if we measure the ratio of private sector in relation to public sector we find that some economies with a large private sector (such as Thailand, Malaysia, and Indonesia) have opted for rehabilitation, whereas others (like Sri Lanka and Taiwan) have opted for the new entry approach.

As has been the case in other markets, the rehabilitation of state-owned banks in Asia has yielded mixed results. Broadly, the four countries where restructuring has been monitored most closely include Indonesia, South Korea, Malaysia, and Thailand (see table 5.3.).

The most successful examples of asset management companies among these Southeast Asian countries include Korea Asset Management Company (KAMCO) and Danaharta (Malaysia). The South Korean government estimates that since the acquisition of nonperforming loans by KAMCO,

Table 5.3   Cross-country outcomes of bank restructuring

Country	Value of assets taken over 1998 (US$ billions)	Asset value as a percentage of GDP	Percent of assets sold 2001
Indonesia	57.8	57	7
South Korea	84.1	11	48
Malaysia	10.3	12	61
Thailand	13.1	11	70

Source: Klingebiel et al., 2001.

nonperforming loans held by banks and other financial institutions has declined to US$69 billion by the end of 1999 from US$84 billion in 1998. Danaharta has carved out 35 percent of total banking system nonperforming loans and has now moved from the acquisition stage to management and disposal of nonperforming loans. Although pricing continues to be a major hindrance to recovery in South Korea and Malaysia, the disposal process remains on track. It is estimated that KAMCO and Danaharta have a recovery rate of 48 and 61 percent of the price value of the amount of debt acquired. By comparison, the RTC in the United States had a recovery rate of 87 percent.

Among the less successful examples of asset management in Asia include Indonesia. The asset management unit of the Indonesia Bank Restructuring Agency (IBRA) has taken over about one-third of total nonperforming loans. The task of recapitalizing banks in Indonesia is largely completed, but has cost the government over US$80 billion (or 57 percent of GDP). Despite some progress in restructuring, Indonesian banks are still saddled with a high level of nonperforming loans (close to 40 percent of total loans).

So far the experience of Chinese AMCs is significantly less favorable than that of the most successful examples shown here. As discussed earlier, there are four AMCs: China Huarong Asset Management Company (CHAMCO), China Orient Asset Management Company (COAMCO), Xinda Asset Management Company (XAMCO), and China Great Wall Asset Management Company (CGWAMCO). By the end of 2001 the outcomes from these different asset management companies varied widely. (See table 5.4.)

Table 5.4 Performance by Chinese asset management companies, 2001

Name of asset management company	Bank holding NPLs	Value of NPLs acquired ($ billions)	Value of NPL disposed ($ billions)	NPL disposed as a proportion of NPL acquired (%)	Recovery rate of NPL disposed (%)
Huarong	ICBC	50.8	0.9	1.9	54
Orient	BOC	33.4	2.4	7.1	46
Great Wall	ABC	43.1	3.1	7.2	NA
Xinda	CCB	43.8	4.7	10.9	33
Total		171.1	11.1		

Source: AMC websites. Available at: www.huarong.com.cn, www.cinda.com.cn, www.gwamcc.com, www.coamc.com.cn.

As table 5.4 shows, the reported recovery rate by each AMC (with the exception of Great Wall) equaled or exceeded 33 percent. Although potentially impressive, the high cash-recovery rate reported by the AMCs must be weighed against a number of factors. First, by 2002, AMCs began to offer more modest claims of the rate of cash recovery. By 2002, all four AMCs claimed to have recovered nearly 22 percent in cash for bad assets. In June 2003, the BOC claimed to have reduced its nonperforming loan ratio to 19.16 percent.

The decline in cash recovery rate could be explained by the probability that the highest quality assets are resolved first. As table 5.4 shows, as the percentage of NPLs disposed increases, the recovery rate declines. Thus, in 2001, Huarong claimed a cash recovery rate of 54 percent, but had merely disposed of 1.9 percent of its NPLs. By the end of 2002, Huarong reported a recovery rate of 32 percent after having settled 7 percent of its NPLs. Any purported progress made by asset management companies in loan restructuring must also be evaluated in light of China's unique willingness to declare restructured loans as being normal loans. According to international accounting standards, restructured loans are classified as being substandard.

In China, credit and money growth are weak because banks are capital constrained and unwilling to lend. So far the modest recovery rates by Huarong and Xinda point to a potential flaw in Chinese AMCs. AMCs in China may not resolve the nonperforming loan problem because it is unlikely that the AMCs detailed before will improve credit quality or increase the size of the potential bank customer base. The AMCs could be a costly warehouse rather than a debt-restructuring agency. The AMCs are likely to transfer the debt burden onto the central government without the benefit of an equal and offsetting boost to growth.

Another factor to consider in asset disposal is the nature of the buyer. Since assets are sold at a substantially lower price than the book value, there is an inherent danger that assets will be sold to domestic institutions with hidden links to the nonperforming loans in question. Alternatively, if distressed assets are made available internationally, it is unclear whether foreign investors would be interested in them as a result of the current prohibition against capital gains repatriation.

The rules regarding disclosure have prompted some banks to seek alternative remedies for loan collection. In August 2001, the BOC's Hong Kong branch has taken the unusual step of suing provincial-level authorities in Shanxi and Xinjiang over loans extended to enterprises backed by their respective provincial governments. Although the dispute revolves around a relatively low amount ($5.5 million in Shanxi and $2.8 million in Xinjiang), the implications could be noteworthy. Since the loans were extended to these enterprises in the mid-1980s, the current litigation signals an intent to collect loans from other creditors. At the same time, the litigation points to the sensitivity of the issue. Currently the BOC has undertaken this action in Hong Kong courts only. Any potential adverse effects are limited to the enforceability of any potential judgment in Hong Kong courts.

The experience in India with loan collection appears to be more promising. The 1985 Sick Industries Companies Act provided so-called sick companies—namely those that have incurred heavy losses—with protection from creditors by the Board for Industrial and Financial Reconstruction. The 1985 Act obviously gave incentives to defaulting companies to incur heavy losses and thus obtain protection from recovery.

In 1993, the passage of the Recovery of Debt Due to Banks and Financial Institutions Act aimed to provide some legal redress to lenders insofar as security enforcement could be obtained through a recovery agent appointed by the courts. Nevertheless, sick industries were protected by the absence of a specific time frame for recovery. Recently, with the passage of the 2002 Securitization and Reconstruction of Financial Assets and Enforcement of Security Ordinance, Indian banks also operate under a legal regime that enables secured lenders to seek recovery of dues by defaulting borrowers after providing a notice of 60 days.

5.4 The Challenges to Optimal Financial Restructuring

Operational restructuring aims to improve a financial institution's profitability. The tools to improve a bank's profitability may include a reduction in operation costs, improved management and accounting techniques, and improved credit assessment. As shown in chapter 4, both Chinese and Indian banks have, with varying degrees of success, some form of operational restructuring.

Although there are no universally accepted standards of what constitutes optimal financial restructuring, a set of international norms appears to be developing. These standards have developed under the supervision of the Basle Committee on Banking Regulation and Supervisory Practices. The Basle Committee is composed of members of the G-10 and Luxembourg. The Basle Committee operates under the auspices of the Bank for International Settlements (BIS). The BIS is the international financial institution that serves as a forum for promoting interbank cooperation. The Basle Committee's most significant report has been the 1988 Capital Adequacy Accord (popularly known as the Basle Accord). The Basle Accord formulated broad supervisory standards and guidelines to be adopted voluntarily by individual countries. Since the work of the Basle Committee is advisory, the 1988 Basle Accord represented the views of all its members. Since 1988, over 100 countries have adopted the norms established by the Basle Accord.

In addition to the Basle Accord, there are other lesser-known international regional groups that promote enhanced international banking supervision. These include the Commission of Latin American and Caribbean Supervisory and Inspection Organization, the Group of Banking Supervision in Arab Countries, and the Southeast Asia, New Zealand, and Australia Forum of Banking Supervision. Since neither China nor India belong to any such international institution, the Basle Committee remains the most notable source of reference on banking issues for most emerging markets.

The Basle Accord intended to ensure that banks had adequate capital to cover credit risks. For that purpose, the BIS has prescribed certain types of capital adequacy standards. One of these standards includes a uniform classification of the calculation of capital. The BIS has popularized the usage of two broad categories to measure capital: Tier 1 and Tier 2 capital. Tier 1 capital consists of share capital and disclosed reserves. Tier 2 capital consists of undisclosed capital and latent reserves, general provisions, hybrid capital, and subordinated debt.

In conjunction with the BIS norms for capital valuation, there are a series of norms to measure capital adequacy. In the United States, the Federal Depository Insurance Company rates the capital adequacy of banks using a broad-based method called CAMEL ratings. CAMEL is an acronym for capital adequacy, asset quality, management ability, earnings record, and liquidity. With CAMEL ratings, capital adequacy is measured using a capital ratio, normally defined as capital divided by assets. In addition, there are other methods of measuring capital adequacy that include measures of risk.

Capital risk asset ratios (CRAR) include broad measures of the total risk-valued capital of depository institutions, which is the ratio of total capital to risk-weighted assets. Another measure of capital risk is the ratio of Tier 1 (or core capital) to risk-weighted assets. Similarly, capital adequacy can be measured as a ratio of Tier 1 capital to total average assets. Finally, capital can be measured as a ratio of tangible capital to total assets. Tangible capital is the sum of Tier 1 capital plus outstanding cumulative preferred stock minus all intangible assets.

The Basle Accord sought to make banks more cautious in their approach to lending. For this purpose, the Basle Accord proposed that internationally active banks could be considered to be adequately capitalized if these institutions could maintain capital to at least an 8 percent level of their risk-adjusted assets. In establishing a benchmark norm of 8 percent of risk-adjusted assets, the BIS proposed establishing a uniform risk-weighting framework that tied capital requirements to credit risk. Thus, a depository institution could be considered to be undercapitalized if it has a total risk-based capital ratio that is less than 8 percent. Depository institutions are considered to be critically undercapitalized if it has a ratio of tangible equity to total assets that is equal to or less than 2 percent.

The issue of capital adequacy of Chinese commercial banks is mandated by statute, namely by the provisions of the 1995 Law on Commercial Banks. Pursuant to Article 38(1) of the 1995 Law, the capital adequacy ratio of commercial banks "may not be lower than 8 percent." As discussed throughout this chapter, the operational accounting standards undertaken in China differ subtly, yet significantly, from the accounting standards proposed by the BIS. Differences in the calculation of capital adequacy ratio are another area in which Chinese banks tend to boost their performance. Chinese banks assign lower risk weights to nonbank loans than are accepted by international accounting standards. Since the bulk of loans by state-owned banks are made toward loss-making SOEs, Chinese banks tend to report a higher CRAR.

In order to remedy this situation, the Ministry of Finance has issued general accounting standards. The accounting standards are officially known as Accounting Standards for Business Enterprises (ASBE). In the first quarter of the year 2000, the Ministry of Finance has attempted to issue a set of strict regulations regarding corporate governance. One of the key elements in these directives include the effort to raise China's accounting standards to international accounting standards. The Ministry of Finance directives also attempt to make provisions regarding other areas of corporate governance by urging listed companies to make more prudent provisions for bad debt and for the valuation of long-term and short-term investments.

The CSRC has also attempted to establish new rules regarding the listing of banks. In addition to the Ministry of Finance's rules regarding transparency, since November 2000 the CSRC has mandated that listed banks disclose their asset quality and internal account mechanisms in their initial public-offering prospectus. In December 2000, the CSRC extended these disclosure requirements to all listed financial stocks. Hence all listed stocks will be required to publish their accounts using criteria from the international accounting standards. The listed banks would also have to disclose information about the precise accounting standards that they use in evaluating their assets and liabilities. In addition, the CSRC has also issued new rules regarding loan provisioning. Newly listed banks are required to provide for adequate write-off and loan provisions.

An associated concern relating to banks is the widespread usage of bank loans to increase certain stock prices. This process of stock market manipulation is colorfully known as "stir frying." The speculative bubble is burst quickly and proceeds from the inflated stocks are sent to overseas bank accounts. Although illegal, the widespread practice has now attracted the attention of Chinese authorities. For this purpose, the CSRC has established a new investigative unit to crack down on stock market manipulation. At the heart of this investigative drive are two listed technology stocks (China Venture Capital (Group) and Yorkpoint S&T).

The CSRC's standards for listed banks are stricter than those currently used by the PBOC. The PBOC requires provision for loan losses to be made for no more than 1 percent of a given bank's year-end loan balance.

So far, only three banks have been directly affected by the new disclosure standards for listed banks. The three banks are the Shanghai Pudong Development Bank, the Shenzhen Development Bank, and the China Minsheng bank. At this stage, it is unclear whether the stricter disclosure requirements for listed banks are purely experimental or whether they will also be applicable to non-listed banks.

In contrast to China, India has had a decade's worth of experience in adopting BIS norms. In 1992, the RBI proposed the introduction of prudential measures in accordance with BIS norms. Foreign banks operating in India were first mandated to reach the minimum 8 percent risk-weighted capital asset ratio by 1993. The RBI then implemented the BIS's prudential norms, by restoring the capital base to public sector banks. Among public sector banks, the improvements in Tier 1 CAR have been notable. In 2000, among 19 commercial banks, 14 had a Tier 1 CAR below 8 percent. Among the State Bank group, only 2 had a Tier 1 CAR below 8 percent. Nine out of 33 scheduled commercial banks had a Tier 1 CAR below 8 percent. Only 5 out of 44 foreign banks had the same ratio.

5.5 *Banking Reform and Capital Market Development*

The experience in India has not been without its critics. In his study of India's banking system, Raje (2000) faults Indian bank regulators and policymakers for calibrating regulatory compliance in adopting the BIS's capital adequacy norms. However, the goal of capital adequacy norms is to facilitate the development of capital markets. Capital markets raise long-term capital for industry through the issuance of securities. In developed countries, capital market activity has benefited from an increase and diversification of new financial instruments. Local governments and firms issue capital market securities. These include municipal bonds, corporate bonds, and equity securities. In the United States, capital market securities include Treasury notes and bonds issued by the federal government. The maturity of capital market securities tends to be over one year.

In emerging markets, though, capital markets tend to be underdeveloped. In the 1980s, China and India had very weak capital markets. Since the 1990s, China and India are an exception. According to Lou (2001: 28), "the relatively small role of capital is not purely a product of market forces but also of administrative decree: the authorities feared that unrestrained capital market development would drain resources from the state commercial banks and used credit plans to set quotas on how much equity and securitized debt can be issued in a given year." With the impact of globalization in the 1990s, the volume of capital market activity has increased dramatically in both India and China.

Overall market capitalization has grown exponentially. As table 5.5 shows, India has outpaced China in terms of overall market capitalization. However, China's market capitalization has grown at a faster rate than India's.

As table 5.5 shows, market capitalization in India has risen from an almost anemic 19 percent of GDP in 1991 to an estimated 37 percent of GDP by 1995. The growth of market capitalization in China is even more remarkable. In 1991, market capitalization as a percentage of GDP amounted to less than 0.6 percent. In 1995, market capitalization as a percentage of GDP grew to 6 percent. Since 1995, market capitalization as a percentage of GDP has skyrocketed in China. In the year 2000, market capitalization has exceeded 53 percent of China's GDP.

The growth of China and India's capital markets reveals a difference in their nature. In India, the growth in capital markets has been institution driven. Specifically, the entry of foreign banks in the market has increased competition for Indian banks. Foreign banks have played a significant role in solving the capitalization problem, in part because their financial strength reduced the risk of a systemic crisis. Moreover, the foreign presence has

Table 5.5 Comparison of market capitalization in India and China, 1991–1995 (figures in US millions)

	1991	1992	1993	1994	1995
India	47,730	65,119	97,976	127,515	127,199
China	2,028	18,255	40,567	43,521	42,055

Source: IFC, *Emerging stock markets factbook*; available at www.ifciltd.com.

helped reduce margins and foster the growth of market segments, such as the retail deposit market. Banks with foreign ownership (defined as having more than 50 percent of capital) accounted for 8 percent of the system's total assets in 1999, up from 4 percent in 1990.

In contrast, in China, the growth in capital markets has been investor driven. As discussed in chapter 4, market speculation by ill-informed investors has served as the catalyst for market capitalization. With the absence of solid institutional foundations, the future outcome of market capitalization in China stands on looser ground.

In addition to capital markets, developing countries have weak money markets. A money market is a market that consists of financial institutions, underwriters, and dealers in credit and money. Money market transactions involve trade in financial assets whose maturity is less than one year. Money market securities include interbank loans, commercial paper, repurchase agreements, and negotiable certificates of deposit. These types of money market securities differ by issuer. Thus, bank holding and finance companies typically issue commercial paper; repurchase agreements are issued by non-depository financial institutions; and certificates of deposit are issued by banks and savings institutions.

Previous work on financial development of developing countries has tended to ignore the role of money markets. Money market instruments are an important component of economic activity because they show the liquidity management of economic actors. Money market instruments also serve as an indirect tool of monetary policy.

The traditional model for a money market is the London Money Market. This particular money market is composed of the Bank of England, deposit banks, discount houses, and the accepting houses. India's money market is modeled after the British model. In India, the core money market activity is the interbank market. Most interbank market transactions in India involve what are termed call money transactions. Call money transactions refer to interbank transactions where money is lent to clearing banks or to discount houses for short periods, sometimes only overnight. Overall, money market activity of this sort is not the sole indicator of financial system maturity. On the other hand, money markets are helpful because they tend to help the development of a secondary market, often driven by the nonfinancial banking intermediaries (NBFI).

During India's recent period of financial system liberalization, an important development in India's money markets has been the establishment of the Discount and Finance House of India (DFHI). The DFHI was set up as a specialized money market institution for the purpose of providing liquidity to money market institutions. This action has led to the development of a secondary market.

The RBI has also introduced measures to develop money markets. The first measure has been to improve the development of short-term money markets with adequate liquidity. In response to the recommendations by the Narasimhan report, an incremental introduction of a Liquidity Adjustment Facility (LAF) was carried out. During the first phases, an interim LAF provided a mechanism for liquidity management through a combination of repos, export credit refinance, and collateral lending facilities supported by open market operations at fixed interest rates. In June 2000, the RBI instituted a full-fledged liquidity adjustment facility.

During the development of the LAF, the Additional Collateralized Lending Facility would be replaced by variable repo auctions. During the second stage in the implementation of LAF, fixed rate repo would be replaced by variable reverse repo rate auctions. During the final stage of the implementation of the LAF, repo operations would be conducted through electronic transfers.

In addition, the RBI has attempted to facilitate short-term liquidity management of money markets. Beginning in May 2000, the RBI recommended that the minimum daily requirement of CRR balances be reduced from 85 to 65 percent. The RBI also decided that money market mutual funds be organized as separate entities rather than operating through money market deposit accounts.

Moreover, banks and nonbanking financial institutions will be allowed to participate in the potentially thriving insurance sector. In 1999, the passage of the Insurance and Development Authority (IDRA) Act opened India's insurance market to foreign investors. Since March 2000, banking and non-banking financial institutions are allowed to set up joint venture companies for the purpose of undertaking insurance business. In order to qualify for this opportunity, participant institutions must have a reasonable level of net non-performing assets (no more than 5 percent of the combined total outstanding leased/hire purchase assets and advances), three years of profitability, and capital risk asset ratio of no less than 12 percent.

Prior to the splitting up of the PBOC, China's money market did not exist during the early reform period because China was still a monobank system. Since then, the development of a money market has experienced a dramatic growth after its inception following the 1984 financial reforms. Transaction volumes of interbank loans and commercial paper have grown substantially in the mid-1990s.

In response to growing market irregularities, the PBOC began to impose limits on interbank transactions. These decrees limited the participation by nonbanking financial institutions in money market transactions. The PBOC also imposed tight limits on terms and the interest rates of interbank loans. Despite these regulations, China's money market continued to be the most deregulated. Hence there was excessive demand for these instruments. As a result of the absence of a well-functioning capital market, money market transactions were used to finance long-term fixed asset investments (primarily in real estate).

In the mid-1990s, ignoring the caps on interest rates, interbank loan interest rates often tripled the official limit of 6 percent. In order to control the staggering speculative growth of money market instruments, the PBOC centralized the operations of the interbank market. Since 1996, interbank lending could only take place within the confines of the central trading system, the China Foreign Exchange Trade System. The primary participants in centralized interbank markets would be commercial banks and other financial institutions authorized by the PBOC.

The 1995 Commercial Banking Law of the People's Republic of China placed restrictions on banks in accordance with BIS norms. For instance, it required that no more than 8 percent of the capital of banks could be risk-adjusted assets. Moreover, the 1995 Commercial Banking Law limited banks from lending more than 10 percent of their capital to any single borrower.

5.6 Revisions to the Basle Accord and Emerging Markets

The Basle Accord norms remain the most widely accepted in the banking industry. One of the emerging problems with the Basle Accord, though, has been growing criticism at the perceived rigidity of the asset classification proposed by the BIS. As a result of criticisms from the international banking community, in June 1999 the BIS proposed a set of redefinitions of the original norms in the Basle Accord. The Basle Committee then released a second consultative document in January 2001. The new document contained proposals for minimal capital requirements, supervisory review, and market discipline.

Initially, the committee's proposed adjustments to the 1988 Accord were due to be published by the end of 2001. Its implementation among member nations was expected to take place by 2004. A committee, under the chairmanship of William McDonough, was entrusted with the task of drafting changes to the Basle Accord. In January 2001, the committee released a draft of its proposals and set a deadline for industry responses. The primary redefinitions to the Basle Accord include a refinement of the existing capital ratios.

Since the January 2001 release of its draft proposals, the McDonough committee received over 250 responses. In general, the proposed changes have received widespread criticism from various sectors. Banking institutions have insisted that the current ratio of capital to risk assets is too blunt. Banks have requested the ability to set their own standards of credit and operational risk.

In response to criticisms by banks, the BIS has also loosened the rules governing credit risk assessment. The BIS is moving in the direction of allowing banks to conduct their own internal risk assessments. Under the new standards, banks would assess their credit risks under the guidance of international credit rating agencies.

Nevertheless, the proposed revisions to the 1988 Accord have given rise to new concerns among central bankers. For instance, the rules designed to reduce the risk of bank failure have come under heavy criticism. A joint letter signed by the heads of American, European, and Japanese central banking associations requested clarification on various proposals by the McDonough's committee. In addition to the industry concerns over the recalibration of credit risk, central bankers have been concerned about the impact of these proposed rules on individual borrowers and small businesses.

One of the principal areas of concern have been the way that operational risk will be treated by the committee. Operational risk concerns the potential for loss arising from a breakdown in policy controls. It also includes human error and transactions costs relating to contractual disputes, systems, and facilities. The letter by the banking association authorities expressed concern that the increased level of capital that banks would have to carry in order to cover operational risk was excessively burdensome.

For instance, the Institute of International Finance (IIF), a leading association representing the interests of financial institutions, argued that by forcing banks to hold more capital, it would raise the cost of compliance. According to the IIF (2001: 7), the new proposals "could create an excessively conservative and costly capital framework that overestimates the amount of risk on banks' balance sheets." In turn, banks would be less competitive than other banking financial institutions that will not be subject to the proposed regulations.

The sharp criticism by industry associations and central bankers in developed countries has forced the McDonough committee to postpone the timeline for the release of its report until the end of 2002. The Basle Committee's most critical challenge will come from less sophisticated banking systems in emerging markets. The proposed rules do not properly address the underlying cause for the growing recurrence of banking crises in emerging markets. As I argued earlier, the phenomenon of globalization has been associated with an increase in banking crises in emerging markets. The first critical factor that makes unsophisticated banking systems vulnerable to crises is the issue of nonperforming assets.

The role of the Basle Accord on the operation of Chinese and Indian banks remains to be seen. The revision of the capital adequacy standards and credit risk assessment may pose a danger to the viability of efforts to reduce nonperforming loans. China's State Council (2000: 1) suggested, "(t)he reform of China's financial system aims to establish a modern financial system facilitating a Chinese-type socialist market economy and a sound financial order." Part of this goal is to be accomplished by significant reform by financial institutions. According to the State Council (2000: 2), these institutions "should be accountable for their own risks, further improve the financial legal system, rectify and standardize financial order in accordance with law, and strengthen construction of internal control systems."

In an unusually candid response to the McDonough committee, the vice chairman of the PBOC, Liu Tinghuan, argued that the proposed minimum target proportion of regulatory capital related to operational risk is excessively high for developing countries, like China, where "operational risk can be very high given the absence of a well-defined legal framework and adequate internal control systems" (PBOC, 2001: 3).

The Indian response to the Basle Committee's Consultative Paper on a New Capital Adequacy Framework was officially undertaken by the RBI. In its response, the RBI (2001a: 14) doubted that the proposed changes to capital adequacy would have universal applicability. The RBI argued that the new accord should "[p]reserve the spirit of simplicity and flexibility to ensure universal applicability including emerging countries."

The RBI also expressed concerns that India's low sovereign credit rating would affect the risk weights of Indian banks. For that reason, the RBI (2001a: 8) proposed that risk weighting of Indian banks "should be de-linked from that of the credit rating of sovereigns in which they are incorporated. Instead, preferential risk weights should be assigned on the basis of their underlying strength and credit worthiness."

5.7 *Conclusion*

In chapter 4 I highlighted the challenges to Indian and Chinese capital markets. In both countries the regulatory burden has been on enhancing the supply side of security offerings by imposing corporate governance rules. In this chapter I focused on the efforts to improve the asset quality of state-owned banks. Both

Chinese and Indian banks have a similar weakness in nonperforming assets. As I have shown here, the preferred policy option in China has been in favor of restructuring state-owned banks through asset management companies. India's approach has been to allow new domestic entrants into the market.

In Sáez (2001) I developed a model of policy preference. I showed why some governments opt for rehabilitation rather than new entry, even though there appears to be greater efficiency gains from new entry. The model was based entirely on an assumption of utility maximization, specifically a political decision-maker's options regarding banking reform. In this basic utility model, decisions regarding reform hinge on public, nonverifiable benefits, or costs of reform.

The utility function depicted the political decision-makers options regarding banking reform. In this model, there are two verifiable events (the choice between rehabilitation or new entry). The political decision-maker's options are bounded by the value of the reform to the policymaker and by the degree of market share of the state sector. The political decision-maker's options range from little to no reform through complete liberalization. These political decision-makers are trying to make government policy outputs as close as possible to their own preferred policies. As is the case with other utility functions, the only behavioral assumptions that I made were that the political decision-makers are rational actors. Moreover, I assumed that political decision-makers have incomplete information about the economic outcome that would result from each alternative.

In general, whenever the value of reform is low, there is an incentive not to reform. Inversely, whenever the value of reform is high, there is a strong incentive to reform. This model accounts for the multiple equilibria between complete reform and no reform. In the cases shown here, the proportion of reform is guided by the degree of market share held by the state sector in a given industry.

In both the Chinese and Indian cases, international standards have loomed over the proposed improvements in banking regulation. Both India and China are unlikely to benefit from the proposed changes to the Basle Accord. By proposing more stringent standards of credit risk assessment, Chinese and Indian banks may not be able to optimally dispose of their current nonperforming assets.

As I have shown in this chapter, India has been able to reduce nonperforming assets in state-owned banks by allowing new domestic entrants into the sector. As such, the state-owned banking sector is more likely to surpass the demanding capital adequacy standards proposed by the Basle Accord. Although the adopted strategy in China has been in favor of restructuring state-owned banks, I suggest that this strategy will not work. Since the underlying cause for the depth of nonperforming assets, namely politically motivated loans, is not likely to go away, Chinese state-owned banks will not be able to legitimately adopt more stringent capital adequacy standards.

CHAPTER 6

Central Bank Independence: A Comparative Perspective

In chapter 5 I examined the strategies that both China and India have adopted to diminish the burden of nonperforming assets held by state-owned banks. I also examined the efforts that Indian and Chinese banks have undertaken in response to growing international norms favoring the optimal financial restructuring of banks. This chapter develops this theme further by evaluating banking reform from the perspective of the central banks.

In his influential book, *Money and Capital in Economic Development*, the famed economist Ronald McKinnon categorized some financial systems as being repressive. According to McKinnon (1973), government intervention in the pricing and allocation of loanable funds inhibits (represses) financial development by depressing real interest rates. The term repressive may appear to be unduly severe, but on closer examination it aptly describes the constraints on economic activity in a free market.

China and India currently exhibit different levels of financial repression. As will be shown in this chapter, the key source of financial repression in both countries differs by the degree of central bank independence. In this chapter I will first delineate some of the basic functions of central banks in developed economies. I will then show how, in the absence of an independent central bank, China's central bank uses a myriad of administrative controls on state-owned commercial banks. In contrast, India's model of an independent central bank effectively curbs the growth in lending policies of commercial banks. These countries' experiences, if ranked by relative progress in resolving institutional constraints to financial sector intermediation, serve as a model to other transition economies.

In China's case, financial repression was centered upon the central bank's use of a credit plan to regulate the supply and allocation of credit as well as interest rate controls. According to Lou (2001: 40–41), the Chinese central bank's credit plan "governed each bank's credit volume directly (in aggregate, by different types of lending, and sometimes by different sectors, subsectors, and even individual borrowers)." As a lender of last resort, China's central bank has provided poor regulatory supervision of state-owned banks. He concluded that China's inadequate banking regulation and supervision as well as weak internal controls of Chinese commercial banks are two of the key causes for its nonperforming loan problem.

The implications of central bank polices on the overall success of banking reform are clear. Eichengreen and Rose (1998) have hypothesized that banking crises in the developing world show a positive correlation to exogenous factors, such as interest rates. In India's case, a model of central bank independence relative to China, the implementation of monetary policy has been altered by changes in administrative controls on state-owned banks, particularly with respect to various forms of interest rate controls. In this chapter, though, I will evaluate the unexpected macroeconomic effects that central bank independence appears to have had in India and China.

6.1 *Central Banking Policies*

The role of central banks varies widely across nations. One of the key objectives of central banks is to control the money supply and credit as well as to maintain price stability. Central banks often achieve these purposes through monetary policy. Monetary policy refers to government action to influence or control the cost and availability of money and credit.

The efficiency of monetary policy depends on the smooth transmission of signals by the central bank. In turn, they depend on the better functioning of the financial sector. The appropriate and flexible policy thrust should recognize a broad range of instruments that could ensure stability of the markets.

Central banks control the money supply with a variety of monetary tools. Monetary policy can be controlled by the central banks with a mix of general and selective tools. General tools aim to control the quality, availability, or cost of money throughout the economy without regard to the purpose of the funds. The most often-used general policy tools are the regulations governing bank reserves. The most illustrative example of general monetary policy is the U.S. Federal Reserve's usage of open-market operations. For instance, the U.S. Federal Reserve buys and sells U.S. government securities with the purpose of increasing or decreasing bank reserves and the money supply. The sale or purchase of government securities by the central bank influences their price. Hence, open market operations of this type tend to have the effect of directly influencing domestic interest rates and the monetary base.

Another significant tool used by central banks to carry out monetary policy is the discount rate. The discount rate is the rate of interest charged by banks and other depository institutions when borrowing funds from the central bank. Since adjustments in the discount rate allow central banks to significantly affect the cost and availability of credit for the general public, it is perhaps one of the most notable tools of monetary policy.

The third principal device used to effectuate monetary goals is the reserve requirement. Reserves are funds that a depository institution must set aside, primarily in the form of deposits. Changes in reserve requirements directly affect the volume of loans and other investments. Typically, a rise in the reserve requirement reduces the money supply. Hence, depository institutions may support and, therefore, have an immediate impact on the availability of credit.

Selective policy tools, on the other hand, focus on specific financial markets or component of total credit, such as stock market lending, consumer credit, or real estate. One of the most common selective policy tools is credit control. Using this technique, the allocation of bank credit may be influenced directly by stipulating the type, amount, and duration of loans that can be made. The purpose of selective policy is to control the cost or flow of funds into selected sectors and to influence the allocation of aggregate expenditure between various sectors of the economy.

Both general and selective policy tools tend to have short-term and long-term effects. Monetary policy tools are inherently blunt instruments of policy. In developed markets, actions from the central bank signal broad macroeconomic policy changes. Due to the rapidity of transactions in the financial markets of developed countries and the lag in the implementation of monetary policy, the desired policy signals from the central bank can be short-circuited by investor actions. The long-term effects of monetary policy in developed markets should not be underestimated. For instance, a modest change in the reserve requirement of banks results in a direct shift in the demand of deposit expansion in the banking system. This shift ultimately affects the growth of the money supply in the economy.

In the financial markets of emerging markets, though, central bank policy serves as a more forceful policy tool. One of the key differences between central banks in developing and developed countries is that monetary policy in developing countries serves to promote specific industrial sectors. Thus, central banks play a disproportionate role in industrial development. As such, central banks in developing countries tend to use selective monetary policy tools. For instance, Mexico's central bank uses its reserve requirement power over commercial banks to direct loans to specific industries and into low-income housing. At the same time, central banks in developing countries face some limitations. Given the absence of a developed securities market, open market operations are circumscribed in developing countries. The limited impact of multiple credit creation in emerging markets also suggests that it is more difficult to bring about changes in the level of credit.

Outside of its role as a regulator of the financial system, central banks play an indirect, yet important role, as agents of fiscal policy. Central banks and other public financial institutions often engage in what have been termed as "quasi-fiscal activities" (QFAs; Mackenzie and Stella, 1996).

The state-owned banking system, though, allows for the enhancement of soft budget constraints by allowing the central government to transfer extra-budgetary funds to subnational jurisdictions. One method of circumventing hard budget constraints is through central bank lending to subnational units at preferred or below-market rates. In a liberalized financial system, banks can make loans to regions with the highest probability of profit. In the transition system, banks can make loans to regions with the highest probability of profit. On the other hand, in transition economies in LDCs, the central government utilizes the state-owned banking system to transfer funds to the least promising regions. Among the selected LDCs, the usage of the state-owned banking system to make extra-budgetary transfers is most critical in China. Several studies have highlighted the role of banks in shaping federal relations in China (Echeverri-Gent, 2000; Sehrt, 2000).

In the case of China and India, the significance of QFAs stem from the central banks dual role as a regulator of the financial system as well as from its role as regulator of the exchange rate system. In its role as a regulator of the financial system, the PBOC and the RBI promote subsidized lending and sectoral credit ceilings. The central bank in both countries acts as the institution that carries out rescue operations of financially troubled institutions. In its role as the regulator of the exchange rate system, the PBOC and the RBI engage in QFAs through multiple exchange rates.

6.2 Expected Outcomes of Central Bank Autonomy

Another key difference between central banks in developed and emerging markets is the degree of autonomy of central banks. The desirability of central bank independence extends to the work of Kydland and Prescott (1977) and the Barro–Gordon (1983) model of time inconsistency. Their work concerned the problems of time inconsistency policy, namely resulting from the lags between policy-induced adjustments and its eventual effect on the economy. In order to alleviate the inflationary bias and to show the credible commitment by governments to provide price stability, several solutions have been proposed. Barro and Gordon (1983) proposed the appointment of reputable central banks. Rogoff (1985) and others have emphasized the need for conservative central banks. Finally, Fischer (1994) proposed greater central bank independence.

Central bank independence can be measured by a number of indices. The most widely used indices of central bank independence are those devised by Grilli et al. (1991) and Cukierman (1994). The independence of central banks can be gauged based on specific institutional arrangements. These include the appointment, length of tenure, and the duties of central bank governors and statutory regulations regarding the scope of the central bank's influence on monetary policy. Some indices are based on the actual turnover of central bank governors. There are also indices that measure independence based on the legal limitations imposed by the charter of central banks.

The autonomy of the central bank has been a recurrent theme in the literature on monetary policy of central banks. There is wide cross-country variation in the central bank's relationship to the central government. In some countries, the central bank is almost viewed as being subordinate to the government insofar as the government determines monetary policy. In developed markets, the Bank of England, the Bank of Japan, and the Bank of France are all examples of central banks that lack independence.

Broadly developed markets tend to have central banks that are independent from other branches of government. The model for an independent central bank is the U.S. Federal Reserve. In the United States, the Board of Governors of the Federal Reserve System is an independent agency that has the discretion to determine the precise means by which monetary policy goals will be achieved, without being subjected to the control of other government officials. In contrast, emerging markets tend to have central banks that lack autonomy from other branches of government.

Aside from political considerations, the decision to have an independent central bank stems from empirical evidence that independent central banks are more likely to stave off inflation and to assure price stability.

In his seminal article, Rogoff (1985) argued that by delegating monetary policy to an independent, conservative central banker the governmental inflationary bias could be reduced, because the primary goal of the conservative central banker would be to stress inflation rate stabilization relative to output stabilization. Other empirical studies also show that among industrialized nations, central bank independence is negatively correlated with inflation (see Blackburn and Christensen, 1989). However, the view that central bank independence necessarily leads to a reduction of inflationary pressures is not universal. A study by Posen (1998) finds no negative correlation between central bank independence and inflation.

Among emerging markets, the benefits of central bank independence are even less certain. Cukierman (1994) showed that central bank independence is not necessarily correlated to inflationary control. However, in less developed countries, the turnover ratio of central bank governors appears to show a strong positive correlation with inflationary control. Moreover, Cukierman has shown that central bank independence is a strong determinant of economic growth in less developed countries. Maxfield (1997) also reached the same conclusion. However, the effect of central bank independence on other sectors of the economy in LDCs does not appear to be supported by empirical studies.

Fry (1996) has argued that central bank independence is determined by the magnitude of the central government's deficit as well as the methods that are used to finance it. Sikken and de Haan (1998) show that there is no relationship between central bank independence and the level of budget deficits.

New analysis of central bank independence using political control variables tends to offer other explanations. According to Wagner (1999), in transition economies, central bank independence can be ineffective or counterproductive if it is merely a legal fiction. Similarly Bagheri and Habibi (1998) show that central bank independence is positively correlated with political freedom and regime stability. This finding is consistent with Moser's (1999) study of OECD countries in which he argued that the negative correlation between inflation and legal central bank independence is strongest in countries with legitimate processes that are characterized by extensive checks and balances as opposed to those that do not have a formal system of governance.

6.3 Central Bank Independence in China and India

China is an example of a country where the central bank lacks autonomy from the government. Prior to the creation of specialized banks, the PBOC acted as the key institution for monetary policy and virtually controlled all lending capacity in China. As discussed in chapter 3, in 1979, the central bank activities of the PBOC were separated from the lending activities of newly created specialized banks and other nonbanking financial institutions. In 1983, a State Council Resolution converted the PBOC into a central bank.

The precise policy functions of the PBOC were not legally established until the passage of the 1986 Provisional Regulations on the Administration of Banks in the PRC. Neither the 1983 Constitution of the PBOC nor the 1986 PBOC Regulations provided clearly defined duties. Under the 1995 Law of the People's Republic of China on the People's Bank of China, the PBOC has precisely circumscribed duties relating to business operations as well as financial supervision and control. Under the 1995 Law, the PBOC was granted legislative authority, under the supervision of China's State Council, to formulate and implement monetary policy. The 1995 Law granted the PBOC specific instruments to implement monetary policy. For instance, under the provisions of Article 22, the PBOC is authorized to set base interest rates and to provide loans for commercial banks. Moreover, the 1995 Law also authorized the PBOC to control the banking industry.

The PBOC's dual function gave rise to a proposed policy reform to delink the PBOC from banking supervision. The effort to separate the PBOC's monetary policy and banking supervision roles—by creating a separate supervisory body—was temporarily abandoned in 2002 when the supervisory functions were allocated to a newly created supervisory bureau within the PBOC. Eventually, in March 2003, an independent regulatory agency, the China Banking Regulatory Commission (CBRC) was created. The CBRC will henceforth be responsible for supervising banks in China. The creation of the CBRC will enable the PBOC to concentrate exclusively on monetary policy.

Despite the supervision by the State Council, the PBOC has some minimal, autonomous operational scope. The PBOC has the legal authority to determine the amount and terms of lending to financial institutions in China. Accordingly, all specialized banks maintain a minimum reserve requirement determined by the PBOC. Moreover, the PBOC has the power to engage in interest rate realignments without the active participation by the State Council. It is unclear at this stage whether the creation of the CBRC will signal that the PBOC will have greater decision making authority on monetary policy issues.

Despite the changes to the status of the PBOC, it ultimately remains an institution that works under the supervision of the State Council. Institutionally, under the provisions of Article 9 of the 1995 Law, the State Council has the power to shape the composition of the leadership of the PBOC. The PBOC has a board of directors that includes a governor, a deputy governor, vice ministers of the Ministry of Finance and various

State Council commissions, a deputy director of the State Planning Committee, and the presidents of the specialized banks. The governor of the PBOC is also the chairman of the PBOC's Board of Directors. The State Council nominates the governor as well as the deputy governors of the PBOC. Although the PBOC can determine the subjects for discussion in its agenda, it is ultimately the State Council that decides all-important questions. To wit, Article 5 of the 1995 Law specifies that the PBOC "shall report its decisions to the State Council for approval concerning the annual money supply, interest rates, foreign exchange rates, and other important matters specified by the State Council before they are implemented." Moreover, as specified in the 1995 Law, the State Council also monitors the operations of the monetary policy committee and supervises the budget of the PBOC.

The future relationship between the State Council and the PBOC is cloaked by ambiguity. The State Council (2000) has announced a significant restructuring of the central bank. It is likely that some of the functions of the central bank will be decentralized to subnational banks. According to the State Council (2000: 2), "(w)ith regard to the central bank's restructuring, a number of trans-province, cross-autonomous region and trans-municipality first-class branch banks will be established in the coming years." The State Council added, "(p)refecture and county-level banks will basically be same, but their functions will be changed" (ibid.).

6.4 *Central Bank Leadership*

A central tenet in the literature on central bank independence is the issue of central bank leadership. An independent central banker, being immune to political pressure, is more likely to have a stable tenure in office. Nonindependent central bankers, being subject to contradictory preference points, are more likely to rotate rapidly.

China's central bank featured an initial pattern of high turnover ratio. The lack of independence of the PBOC has prompted volatility in the top leadership position of the PBOC. For instance, the first governor of the PBOC, Lu Peijian, was appointed in 1984. A year later Lu Peijian was replaced by Chen Muhua. Chen Muhua's tenure was equally short-lived as she resigned in 1988. This period of instability in the leadership of the PBOC ended with Zhu Rongji, when he became the governor of the PBOC in 1993.

The redefinition of the jurisdiction of the PBOC under the 1995 Law has added an element of stability in the leadership of the PBOC. Until January 2003 the central bank governor was Dai Xianglong. He served as the senior vice governor of the PBOC while Zhu Rongji was the governor of the PBOC. In this sense, the close working relationship between Zhu Rongji and Dai Xianglong has helped to overcome the institutional instability inherent in a nonindependent central banker. Dai Xianglong's replacement, Zhou Xiaochuan, has a reputation for being a more aggressive reformer. At this stage it remains to be seen whether Zhou Xiaochuan will enjoy the same level of access as that of his predecessor.

One of the main reforms of the PBOC under the leadership of Dai Xianglong has been to support financial reforms that would enable the liberalization of its domestic interest rate regime. The liberalization of interest rates has been deemed to be the optimal precondition toward eventual convertibility of China's currency, the renminbi. The complete liberalization of interest rates is expected to take at least three years. The central bank then aims to liberalize rates on rural credit followed by liberalization in urban areas. Dai Xianglong's successor has also made interest rate liberalization, together with exchange rate reform, his top priority.

The weakness of consumer lending has prompted China's central bank to take some measures. The China Construction Bank has been authorized by the central bank to issue mortgage-backed debts. Mortgage-backed securities are drawn from a pool of mortgage loans. The monthly payments of principal and interest from this pool of mortgages are then passed on to the holders of the securities. These securities tend to minimize a bank's risk as it extends housing loans. In line with China's approach to experimentation of public policy at the local level, the China Construction Bank is expected to start this process in the cities of Shenzhen and Guangzhou.

The liberalization of interest rates could be signaled by an expansion of the floating band of lending rates. On March 16, 2002, in a speech before the Bank of China Forum held in Beijing, Dai Xianglong hinted that the PBOC "shall proceed steadily with interest rates liberalization." In order to accomplish this goal, he argued, "the first step is to increase the band by setting a minimum lending rate or a ceiling for deposit rates. Secondly, open market operations will have a larger role to play" (PBOC, 2002).

Among developed economies, central bank independence is a feature of the Federal Reserve System in the United States and the Bundesbank in Germany. India is an example of an independent central bank. As was discussed in chapter 3, the development of India's central banking system was marked by three distinctive phases. The first phase was the establishment of the three presidential banks. The second stage was the overall amalgamation of these three existing presidency banks into the Imperial Bank. The final stage was the establishment of the RBI.

The RBI was created with the passage of the 1934 Reserve Bank of India Act. According to the Preamble of the 1934 Act, the purpose of the RBI was "to regulate the issue of bank notes and the keeping of reserves with a view to securing monetary stability in British India and generally to operate the currency and credit system to its advantage." The RBI began operations in 1935. A clear limitation of the duties of the existing Imperial Bank and the Governor-General-in-Council was that the primary function of the RBI was the regulation of the issuance of bank notes with the intent of improving the overall monetary policy framework. According to Section 22(1) of the 1934 Act, the RBI "shall have the sole authority right to issue bank notes in British India."

Since the RBI was created during the period of British rule in India, the central bank closely followed the structure of the Bank of England. Until the RBI was nationalized in 1949, it differed from the Bank of England in that the entire share capital of the RBI was largely owned by private shareholders. Moreover, the RBI's initial statutory obligations did not grant it comprehensive powers over other Indian banks.

The current statutory powers of the RBI emanate from the Banking Companies Act of 1949. Section 21 of the 1949 Act granted the RBI comprehensive powers of supervision over India's banking system. Under the provisions of this section, the RBI was to handle the currency programs of the central and the state governments. In addition, it acted as a backer to commercial banks, state cooperative banks, and some fund institutions. Aside from the powers listed in Section 21 of the Act, Section 22 of the Act empowers the RBI to grant licenses to new banks.

Under the provisions of Section 10A of the 1949 Banking Regulation Act, the RBI operates under the guidance of a central board of directors. The institutional structure of the central board of directors is simple. The governor exercises the executive authority of the RBI. Three deputy governors, each of whom is in charge of a certain role of the RBI, assists the RBI's governor. These sections include note issuance, banking operations, and rural credit. The governor and the deputy governors serve five-year terms, but are eligible for reappointment.

The function of the RBI was expected to include the normal functions of a central bank relating to general credit control. A central theme in the RBI's approach to monetary policy has been price stability and inflation control. Interest rate liberalization in India is part of the overall financial reform that has been implemented on a gradual basis since the early 1980s. The early stage of the reform has been rather selective, mostly in response to specific problems in each period.

The financial liberalization program could have been pursued more aggressively in the second half of the 1980s, if it had not been for the serious macroeconomic problems as well as the financial system crisis facing India during that period. On the external front, India's current account deficits increased from 1.2 percent of GDP in 1985 to 3.1 percent in 1990. Total foreign exchange reserves declined by 25 percent from 1990 to 1991. Similarly, foreign currency assets were depleted by 63 percent in the same time period. Domestically, several leading financial institutions also faced severe liquidity shortages and fundamental insolvency. The Indian authorities' main concern in the latter half of the 1980s was to restore macroeconomic and financial stability.

In order to cope with the external imbalance, liberalization in structural adjustment measures was taken. Manmohan Singh undertook India's structural adjustment measures. He last served as the governor of the RBI from 1982 to 1985. His previous government experience was instrumental in India's quick recovery. As finance minister, Manmohan Singh promoted a set of specific structural adjustment measures. These included current and capital account liberalization, and a dramatic restraint on central government expenditures. Other measures included the liberalization of imports and a 15 percent devaluation of the rupee in 1995.

Manmohan Singh's stabilization and structural adjustment measures have proven to be effective in reversing the external imbalance and stimulating growth. Current account receipts have increased from 8 percent of GDP in 1991 to 15.3 percent in 2000. Current account deficits declined from an average of 1.75 percent of GDP during 1985–1990 to 1.24 percent of GDP during 1995–2000. Real economic growth also increased from an average of 5.85 percent during 1985–1990 to 6.6 percent during 1995–2000.

Since India's independence from British rule, the RBI has benefited from a legacy of continued leadership. Over the last 20 years, three RBI governors have played an important leadership role in the RBI. They include R.N. Malhotra (1985–1990), C. Rangarajan (1992–1997), and Bimal Jalan (1997-present).

R.N. Malhotra initiated India's first successful efforts at banking reform through a streamlining of selective credit controls. The relaxation of minimum margin requirements allowed banks to fix their own short-term deposit rates within a ceiling rate not exceeding 8 percent of total assets. This policy met with considerable opposition and had to be partially reversed by the Ministry of Finance.

C. Rangarajan took over the helm of the RBI during India's most critical economic periods in the formation of India's capital markets. Rangarajan took a keen interest in the improvement of corporate governance of India's banks and nonbanking financial institutions. In an assessment of the improvements to corporate governance in India under his leadership, Rangarajan (1997) pointed to the establishment of a Board for Financial Supervision in November 1994. The purpose of the Board was to provide prudential supervision to commercial banking and financial institutions.

Moreover, Rangarajan highlighted the appointment of a committee to review the internal control and inspection audit functions within banks. According to Rangarajan (1997: 790), improved prudential norms for income organization and asset classification would enhance the overall credibility of the financial system. Rangarajan added that the "(e)arnings are substantially affected by the quality of assets and it is for this reason that the (prudential) norms focus on the quality of assets and on upgrading capitalization."

The principal policy issue faced by Bimal Jalan has been the question of weak banks. During his tenure, a concept of narrow banking was proposed. Narrow banking refers to the methods by which faltering banks lower their risk assets by investing in short-term government securities. This policy makes banking run-proof, but also has the tendency to curb one of banks' key functions, the creation of liquidity.

Under Bimal Jalan's tenure, the RBI set up a committee to offer recommendations on how to revive weak banks. A Working Group, chaired by M.S. Verma, offered an exhaustive list of recommendations. The Verma Committee identified three areas as being critical to the successful recovery of weak banks. These areas were solvency, earning capacity, and profitability. The Verma Committee rejected the adoption of narrow banking as the sole, long-term restructuring strategy. Instead it proposed that weak banks be restructured in a two-stage process. During the first stage of the restructuring process, the competitive efficacy of banks would be restored through operational, organizational, and financial restructuring. Long-term restructuring would be followed by a second stage in the restructuring process that would involve complete privatization or merger of restructured banks.

6.5 *Macroeconomic Policy Outcomes in China and India*

The theoretical literature on central bank independence appears to have predicted three outcomes: a reduction in inflation, an increase in economic growth, and budget deficit reduction. As I discussed earlier, Moser (1999) found a negative correlation between central bank independence and inflation; Cukierman (1994) and Maxfield (1997) correlated increases in central bank independence with positive economic growth; and Fry (1996) found

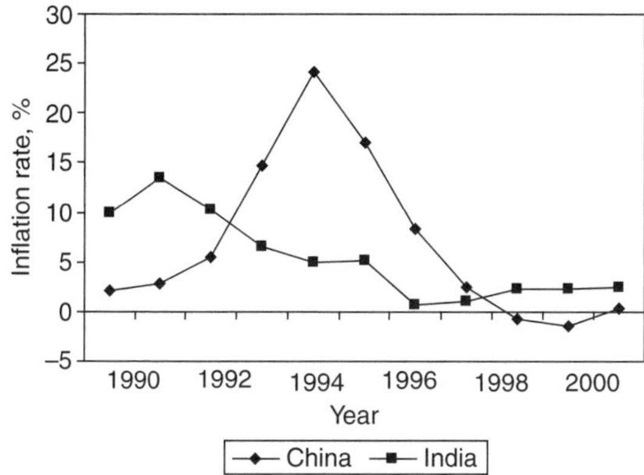

Chart 6.1 Inflation rates in China and India, 1991–2000.

Source: International Monetary Fund, *World Economic Outlook*, May 2001.

a positive correlation between central bank independence and budget deficit reduction.

The examples of China and India provide some concrete lessons that can be drawn regarding the need for central bank independence in emerging markets. However, the evidence for China and India appears to contradict the expected macroeconomic outcomes of central bank independence.

The data on inflation for China and India does not appear to support the contention that central bank independence contributes to a reduction in inflation rates. Chart 6.1 illustrates the rate of inflation for China and India from 1991 to 2000.

Chart 6.1 shows that China experienced a period of a sharp increase in inflation from 1992 to 1994. This period was followed by a steady decline in inflation rates, culminating with negative rates of inflation in 1998 and 1999.

Moreover, central bank independence does not appear to have decreased interest rates. In India there has been a dramatic increase in the prime lending rate from 1991 to 2001. In contrast, China has had a steady increase in the prime lending rate from 1991 to 1995. Since 1995, though, prime lending rates in China have declined dramatically as well (see chart 6.2). As chart 6.2 shows, the peak in prime lending rates in China is equivalent to India's prime lending rate in 2001.

The relationship between central bank independence and rates of economic growth also do not appear to be supported by the experiences of China and India. Despite the lack of central bank independence, China has

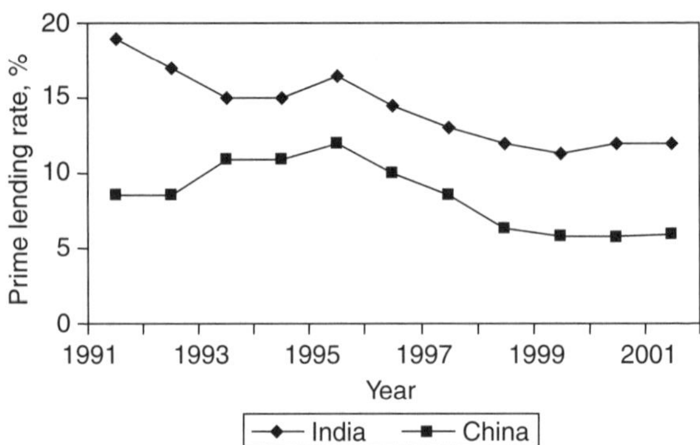

Chart 6.2 Prime lending rates in China and India, 1991–2001.

Source: Jardine Fleming, 2001. Leading indicators, regional strategy.

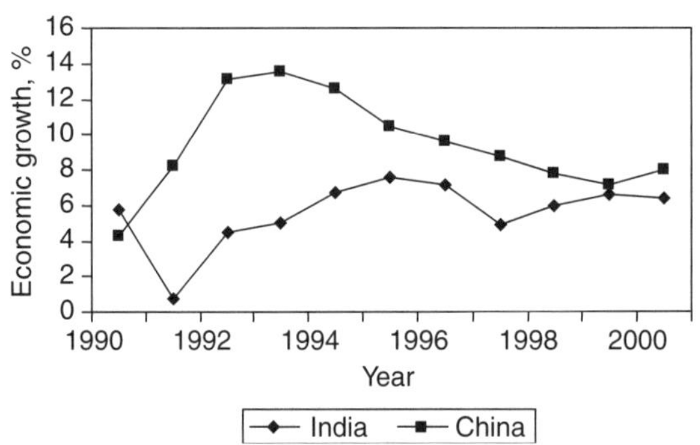

Chart 6.3 Percentage change in gross domestic product in India and China, 1990–2000.

Source: International Monetary Fund, *World Economic Outlook*, 2001.

had one of the world's fastest rates of economic growth. In contrast, India has experienced more modest rates of economic growth (see chart 6.3).

Chart 6.3 indicates that India experienced a sharp drop in GDP growth during its 1991 balance of payments crisis. It has experienced a gradual recovery since. In contrast, China has reported spectacular rates of economic growth, dipping slightly during the 1997 East Asian financial crisis.

Finally, the experiences of China and India suggests that central bank independence is not positively correlated with fiscal deficit reduction. As chart 6.4 shows, China has had a sterling record of fiscal deficit reduction.

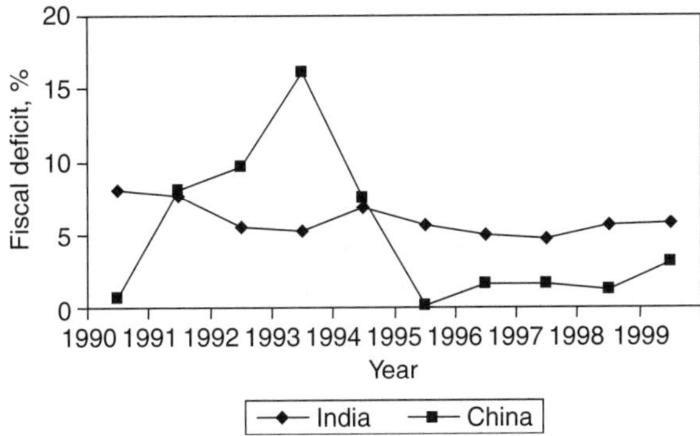

Chart 6.4 Central government fiscal balance for India and China, 1990–2000.
Source: International Monetary Fund, 2000; International Financial Statistics.

As chart 6.4 indicates, India has had a steady reduction of central government fiscal deficits in the 1990s. In contrast, China had a rapid rise in fiscal deficits in the early part of the 1990s. Equally swift was China's ability to diminish its fiscal deficits after the enactment of the 1994 tax rationalization measures.

6.6 Conclusion

This chapter has discussed banking reform through the framework of central bank independence in China and India. In these two countries, the central bank plays a central role in the regulation and supervision of commercial banks. As I have shown in this chapter, confirming the criteria used in Grilli et al. (1991) and Cukierman (1992), the virtual absence of central bank independence in China, relative to India, has been exemplified by the high turnover of central bank leadership. India's higher degree of central bank independence has enabled the RBI to undertake and implement a wider range of both general and selective policy tools.

Paradoxically, the experiences of China and India appear to contradict some of the expected macroeconomic outcomes of central bank independence, particularly those found in Rogoff (1985) and Blackburn and Christensen (1989). In this chapter I have shown that, in China and India, central bank independence is not correlated to inflationary control, largely confirming Cukierman's (1994) finding regarding the purported benefits of central bank independence. Likewise, an increase in central bank independence in China and India has not corresponded with increases in economic growth or budget deficit reduction.

Although these two isolated cases do not necessarily form a pattern among all banking systems in developing countries, these two cases suggest that the promotion of specific policies relating to central bank independence should be examined on a country by country basis. The Chinese case shows that the absence of stability in leadership in a nonindependent central bank can be overcome through noninstitutional linkages.

CHAPTER 7

Repairing Heaven?

The state has traditionally held a critical role in the governance of economic relations in India and China. In China, the organisms of the state were referred to as *tian* (heaven). Despite the central role of the state in governance, challenges to its effectiveness have been dramatic. One of the pivotal episodes in twentieth-century Chinese history was the presentation of Japan's 21 demands to China in 1915. President Yüan Shih-kai dissolved the first parliament of the Republic in 1914 and annulled the Constitution of 1912. He later issued an order for the whole country to worship heaven and Confucius. The demands served as the backdrop for the Japanese occupation of Manchuria.

The Chinese government's response to this humiliation sparked a student protest movement called the May Fourth Movement. This intellectual movement served as the precursor to the development of various socialist and anarchist ideologies in China. Faced with the visible weakness of the Chinese state, the May Fourth Movement began as an anti-Japanese protest, but emerged as an attack on the legitimacy of the state and rule by warlords. During the May Fourth Movement there were intense iconoclastic intellectual debates as to whether heaven (i.e. the state) ought to be repaired (*butian*) or whether heaven should be dismantled (*chaitian*).

The question whether economic reform could be achieved through gradual social reform or through revolution has reemerged in this book, largely with a focus on the banking sector. Following the aftermath of the 1997 East Asian financial crisis, the Chinese and the Indian states were faced with a choice: to dismantle or repair their state-owned banks. China and India are interesting case studies because they are the two most prominent emerging markets that have undertaken banking reforms to prevent a financial crisis.

This process is in sharp contrast with other developing countries that have attempted to reform their state-owned banking systems after the East Asian financial crisis.

So far I have described the process and challenges to banking reform in India and China. In the first section of the book (chapters 2 and 3) I described the historical developments in the institutionalization of the banking system in both countries. In the case of China, a notable feature has been the virtual absence of a private banking system since 1949. Although India has also limited the growth of the private banking sector, largely through nationalization of some of India's largest commercial banks and currently through a licensing process, the development of a domestic private banking sector may have deep repercussions in the resolution of the problem of nonperforming loans held by state-owned banks.

In chapters 2 and 3 I outlined the scope of China and India's institutional arrangements. Institutionally China and India differed from each other in several important respects. First, the degree of market concentration of the state-owned banking system is much higher in China than in India. Despite the existence of a more diversified banking system in India, the role of the state in the commercial banking system remains strong.

The initial emphasis of the reform of the banking system in China concentrated on infrastructure investment, household savings, and consumer lending. Following the widely anticipated accession of China to the WTO, the imminent changes to the degree of foreign participation in the Chinese banking sector have propelled a third set of reforms. In contrast, the initial steps for banking reform undertaken in India have focused on an improvement of the operational restructuring of the state-owned commercial banking system. Hence the policy reforms have focused on interest rate policy, institutional restructuring, and efforts to deal with the problem of state-owned bank overstaffing.

During my analysis of China and India's banking institutions, I highlighted the gradual opening up of China's banking system to foreign competition. Despite India's concerns about the proper role of a domestic private banking industry in a planned economy, foreign banks have operated in India with a great deal of latitude. The experience of India with foreign-bank entry suggests that foreign-bank entry in China will have a far more limited impact than widely anticipated.

In chapters 2 and 3, which introduced the basic institutional features of the Chinese and Indian banking systems, I suggested that the more pronounced presence of domestic private banks in the Indian banking system could spell a solution to the critical problem of nonperforming assets. In the absence of such entry by private sector entities, the state-owned commercial bank in China, and to a lesser extent in India, is hindered from improving its operational structure. In the Chinese banking reform efforts, the emphasis has been on safeguarding prudential regulation of state-owned commercial banks, particularly in its dealings with state-owned enterprises.

Even under ideal circumstances, the prudential regulation of banks is difficult because unlike most other types of intervention, which seek to create and sustain values that result from transacting in the market, this is designed to prevent panics and crises. Given the severe problem of nonperforming assets in the most dominant state-owned commercial banks in China, prudential regulation could force Chinese SOEs to liquidate new stocks in order to repay debt. The other alternative is that they declare bankruptcy.

Chinese policymakers face the additional burden that negative spillovers from SOE reform can threaten the stability of the Chinese regime. Massive layoffs have strained social relations. Presented with these two options, it is likely that there will be a rise of bankruptcies; hence this aspect of banking reform could prove to be contractionary for China.

In contrast, banking reform in India, although initiated by an attempt to reform Indian public sector enterprises, could be expansionary because Indian parastatals are in the process of being privatized. Subjecting the state-owned commercial banking system to greater market discipline should improve the role of public enterprises in overall economic activity. Some of the reforms discussed in this book have attempted to improve the operating environment of banks, but are also likely to spill over to enhance the efficiency of state-owned enterprises in general.

In chapter 4, however, I showed that the problems of corporate governance are not confined to SOEs alone. Despite the rapid growth in the development of financial markets, substandard corporate governance remains a serious obstacle to the development of financial markets in China and India.

In this book I showed that despite the promise of greater openness to foreign financial institutions, China's existing regulatory framework will make it improbable for foreign banks to occupy a sizable market share there. The ambivalence toward the development of a potent domestic private industry and the lingering concerns about foreign-bank entry suggests that transition economies like China and India have yet to fully come to terms with a diminishing responsibility of the state in economic affairs. This tension is later developed more fully in chapter 4 of this book. There I showed the differing patterns that China and India have taken in relation to improved corporate governance.

Within the context of the state's ambivalence toward the private banking sector (whether domestic or international), the likelihood of success in improvements in corporate governance are in question. In China the state has been the engine of reform, whereas in India, the private sector has sought out improved corporate governance rules. In chapter 4 of this book I showed that China has attempted to improve the corporate governance of firms through greater exposure to market discipline. For this reason, China is undergoing a dramatic change in the development of its capital markets.

Once again, the example of India, with its more developed capital markets, shows that market exposure alone will not necessarily lead to an improvement in corporate governance. Paradoxically, the efforts by the Indian state to improve corporate governance by establishing more precise rules regarding trading, mergers, and acquisitions have in themselves created new incentives to engage in corporate malfeasance. The recurring financial scandals that have beset India's stock markets since 1991 will certainly be replicated in China.

The concerns about the improvement of the corporate governance of firms in India and China were later linked more explicitly to the state-owned banking sector. In chapter 5, I showed that the improvement of corporate governance is exogenous to the resolution of the nonperforming asset problem in state-owned banks. I have shown that India has attempted to tackle its problem with nonperforming assets by allowing new entrants into the economy. In contrast, China has attempted to rehabilitate its state-owned commercial banks by way of asset management institutions. In this book I have suggested that new entry approaches appear to have had a more beneficial impact in reducing nonperforming assets. Many governments, however, have opted for the less successful rehabilitation approach.

This book has shown how China and India pursued different paths to banking reform. The banking reforms pursued in China and India has also addressed the problem of nonperforming loans and accumulated losses by state-owned commercial banks. In chapter 5, I focused on the divergent strategies for financial restructuring pursued in China and India. In this book I argued that the penetration of the commercial banking system by domestic private banks could be an example to other emerging markets of successful bank restructuring.

In chapter 5, I suggested that the value of reform to policymakers depends on the market share of the state in a given sector of the economy. The case for shifting the emphasis from supervision to incentives by making failure more costly for management and shareholders of state-owned banks remains to be made. As the cases of China and India show, a contingent liability system and a through structured supervision framework needs to be developed. Moreover, additional cross-national research needs to be conducted to determine whether the value of reform to policymakers depends on the market share of the state in a given sector of the economy.

In chapter 6, I concluded with a paradoxical examination of the macroeconomic outcomes relating to central bank independence. The theoretical literature on central bank independence tends to correlate central bank autonomy with rapid economic growth, lower rates of inflation, and greater fiscal discipline. However, the evidence from China and India appears to point in a different direction. Despite having a nonindependent central bank, toward the latter part of the 1990s, China has clearly outperformed India in its economic growth, inflation rates, and the degree of fiscal discipline.

The comparison of reforms in China and India is interesting to students of international political economy for several reasons. China and India have had similar developmental patterns. Unlike other transition economies in Eastern Europe and Latin America, China and India opted to adopt gradual economic reforms. Although China and India's approach to economic reform has been quite similar, their outcome has been radically different. China reported unprecedented levels of continuous economic growth. China is the world's second largest recipient of foreign direct investment. In contrast, while pursuing similar economic reforms, India has experienced modest levels of economic growth and has attracted modest levels of foreign direct investment.

The probability of certain types of banking reform cannot be explained solely in terms of piece-rate incentives or the expectation of patronage between principals and agents. Otherwise, reform would either be uniform across industrial sectors or it would be greater in those industries where there is an expectation of rent-seeking payoffs. In addition, the incentive of state actors to engage in predatory behavior to deter new entrants is substantially enhanced in monopoly or near-monopoly environments.

In this book I have suggested that the value of banking reform is low whenever there is low dispersal and high concentration of state ownership in the banking sector. The case of China illustrates that modest reform of state-owned commercial banks (in the form of gradual rehabilitation) has taken place in an environment where there is an oligopoly by four state-owned commercial banks. The incentives for continued vertical integration are notable in light of such market imperfection.

The potential costs of reform are great when there is great concentration in the state sector. However, in the face of uncertain outcomes, a policymaker's utility gains outweigh the potential efficiency gains by allowing new entrants into the financial sector. This approach has been replicated in Thailand, Malaysia, and Indonesia.

In contrast, in the absence of complete reform through total privatization, countries where there is high dispersal and comparatively low concentration by the state in a given industrial sector will have an incentive to reform that sector more rapidly. Although the state sector inevitably introduces imperfection into the market, it nonetheless operates in the realm of a quasi-competitive environment. The incentive to reduce the transaction costs of multiple competing SOEs facilitates reform. Moreover, the incentive to engage in predatory behavior to deter new entrants into the market is weakened by virtue of having multiple state actors not reacting in unison. The case of India showed that modest reform of state-owned commercial banks (in the form of allowing new entrants into the economy) takes place where the domain of the state is more diluted in a given sector of the economy.

As argued in Sáez and Yang (2001), the range of individuals who have an impact on the decision to undertake reform in a given sector of the economy is larger in India than in China. This difference reflects the distinctive political regime types in these two countries. The expected cost of sectoral reform can be expressed using public choice terminology. Reform in China is different from reform in India because there are fewer individuals whose agreement is required for reform.

In India, but especially in China, there are hidden debates within the bureaucracy as to the proper steps to undertake in order to formulate and implement the different facets of banking reform examined in this book. An optimal majority is reached when the expected utility loss of reform corresponds to a minimal decision-time costs of achieving the necessary majority in order to enact a reform.

In 1997, some of the most dynamic economies of the world experienced a devastating financial crisis. The East Asian financial crisis had widespread repercussions and lingering effects in other parts of the world. Analysts have attempted to explain how and why the financial crisis occurred at all. The financial crisis revealed that a growing economy could not be sustained with a weak banking infrastructure. The literature that emerged after the East Asian financial crisis has not examined how another financial crisis of this magnitude can be averted.

The two largest developing countries in the world, India and China, are currently experiencing some of the symptoms that bedeviled Malaysia, Thailand, and Indonesia prior to their respective financial crises. Some estimates calculate that bank debts and nonperforming loans of China's state-owned banks amount to nearly 30 percent of China's GDP. Similarly India is also facing a banking crisis. Given the substantial presence of American and European firms in China and India, a financial crisis could have devastating repercussions globally.

References

Official Documents, Laws, and Statutes

Central Committee, Chinese Communist Party. 1993. Decisions by the Central Committee of the Chinese Communist Party on Various Issues Concerning the Establishment of a Socialist Market Economic System. (Adopted by the Third Plenary Session of the Fourteenth Congress of the Chinese Communist Party).

The Indian Central Banking Enquiry Committee, 1931. Vol. I–IV. Calcutta: Government of India Central Publications Board.

Government of India. 1934. Reserve Bank of India Act, 1934. Act No. 2 of 1934.

——. 1936. Indian Companies (Amendment) Act, 1936. Act No. 22 of 1936.

——. 1946a. Banking Companies (Inspection) Ordinances, 1946. Ordinance No. 4 of 1946.

——. 1946b. Banking Companies (Restriction of Branches) Act, 1946. Act No. 27 of 1946.

——. 1949a. Banking Regulation Act, 1949. Act No. 10 of 1949.

——. 1955. State Bank of India Act, 1955. Act No. 23 of 1955.

——. 1959. State Bank of India (Subsidiary Banks) Act, 1959. Act No. 38 of 1959.

——. 1964. Industrial Development Bank of India Act, 1964. Act No. 18 of 1964.

——. 1976. Regional Rural Banks Act, 1976. Act No. 21 of 1976.

——. 1984. Industrial Reconstruction Bank of India Act, 1984. Act No. 62 of 1984.

——. 1995. Banking Companies (Payments and Transfer of Undertakings) Amendment Act, 1995. Act No. 8 of 1995.

——. 1997. Reserve Bank of India (Amendment) Act, 1997. Act No. 23 of 1997.

Government of the People's Republic of China. 2001. *Laws and Regulations of the People's Republic of China.* Vol. I–XVI. Compiled by the Legislative Affairs Committee of the State Council. Beijing: Legal Publishing House.

Hilton–Young Commission of 1926.

Industrial Development Bank of India, General Regulations, 1994. Notification F. No. 1409.

National People's Congress. 1998. Securities Law of the People's Republic of China. (Adopted at the Sixth Meeting of the Standing Committee of the Ninth National

People's Congress on December 29, 1998, and promulgated by Order 12 of the President of the People's Republic of China on December 29, 1998).

National People's Congress. 1988. Law of the People's Republic of China on Industrial Enterprises Owned by the Whole People. (Adopted by the First Session of the Seventh National People's Congress on April 13, 1988, and promulgated by Order 3 of the President of the People's Republic of China on April 13, 1988).

———. 1995. Law of the People's Republic of China on Commercial Banks. (Adopted by the Thirteenth Meeting of the Standing Committee of the Eighth National People's Congress on May 10, 1995, and promulgated by Order 47 of the President of the People's Republic of China on May 10, 1995).

———. 1995. Insurance Law of the People's Republic of China. (Adopted by the Fourteenth Meeting of the Standing Committee of the Eighth National People's Congress on June 30, 1995, and promulgated by Order 51 of the President of the People's Republic of China on June 30, 1995).

———. 1995. Law of the People's Republic of China on Negotiable Instruments. (Adopted by the Thirteenth Meeting of the Standing Committee of the Eighth National People's Congress on May 10, 1995, and promulgated by Order 49 of the President of the People's Republic of China on May 10, 1995).

———. 1995. Law of the People's Republic of China on the People's Bank of China. (Adopted at the Third Session of the Eighth National People's Congress on March 18, 1995, and promulgated by Order 46 of the President of the People's Republic of China on March 18, 1995).

People's Bank of China. 2001. Letter from Liu Tinghuan to William McDonough, dated May 30. Beijing: Information Office, People's Bank of China.

People's Bank of China. 2002. "China's Monetary Policy in the Coming Years." Speech by Governor Dai Xianglong at the Bank of China Forum (March 16), Beijing. Available at http://www.pbc.gov.cn.

———. 1995. General Rules on Loans (Trial Implementation).

Regulations for Changing Over the Operational Mechanism of Enterprises Owned by the Whole People, 1992.

Report of the Committee on the Financial System (Narasimham Committee Report, Bombay 1991). New Delhi: Standard Publications.

Reserve Bank of India. Nationalized Banks (Management and Miscellaneous Provisions) Scheme, 1970. Notification No. S.O. 3793.

———. Nationalized Banks (Management and Miscellaneous Provisions) Scheme, 1980. Notification No. S.O. 875 (E).

State Council. 2000. Regulations on Financial Assets Management Companies. (Adopted at the 32nd Executive Meeting of the State Council on November 1, 2000, and promulgated by Decree No. 297 of the State Council of the People's Republic of China on November 10, 2000).

State Council. 1994. Regulations of the People's Republic of China on Administration of Foreign Financial Institutions with Foreign Capital. (Adopted at the 14th Executive Meeting of the State Council on January 7, 1994, and promulgated by

Decree No. 148 of the State Council of the People's Republic of China on February 25, 1994).

Books and Monographs

Abel, I., Siklos, P., and Szekely, I. 1998. *Money and finance in the transition to a market economy*. Northampton, Massachusetts: Edward Elgar.

Bandyopadhyaya, K. 1976. *Agricultural development in China and India*. New Delhi: Wiley Eastern.

Beijing Institute of International Finance. 1993. *The banking system of China*. Beijing: China Planning Press.

Bhalla, A.S. 1992. *Uneven development in the Third World: A study about China and India*. London: McMillan.

Bhatt, V.V. 1995. *Financial systems, innovations, and development*. New Delhi: Sage Publications.

Byrd, W. 1983. *China's financial system: The changing role of banks*. Boulder, Colorado: Westview Press.

Cable, V. 1995. *China and India: Economic reform and global integration*. London: Royal Institute of International Affairs.

Caprio, G., Honohan, P., and Stiglitz, J. 2001. *Financial liberalization: How far, how fast*. Cambridge: Cambridge University Press.

Centre for Monitoring Indian Economy (CMIE) 2000. *Money and Banking*. Bombay: CMIE.

Chen, B., Dietrich, J.K., and Fang, Y. 2000. *Financial reform in China*. Boulder, Colorado: Westview Press.

Chen, I.K. and Uppal, J.S. (Eds.). 1971. *Comparative Development of India and China*. New York: Free Press.

China Securities and Futures Statistical Yearbook (CSFSY). 2000. Beijing: China Statistical Publishing House.

Cho, Y.J. 2002. *The banking system of the People's Republic of China*. Manila, Philippines: Asian Development Bank.

Choksi, A. and Papageorgiou, D. (Eds.). 1986. *Economic liberalization in developing countries*. London: Basil Blackwell.

Collis, M. 1965. *Wayfoong: The Hong Kong and Shanghai banking corporation*. London: Faber and Faber Limited.

Cukierman, A. 1992. *Central bank strategy, credibility, and independence*. Cambridge, Massachusetts: MIT Press.

Deb, K. 1988. *Indian banking since Independence*. New Delhi: Ashish Publishing House.

Dethier, J.J. (Ed.). 2000. *Governance, decentralization, and reforms in China, India, and Russia*. Boston: Kluwer Academic Publishers.

Deutsche Bank. 2000. *China's local stock market*. Hong Kong: Asia-Pacific Equity Research.

Dzever, S. and Jaussaud, J. (Eds.). 1999. *China and India: Economic performance and business strategies in the mid-1990s.* New York: St. Martin's Press.

Gee, W. and Lau, H. 1999. *Bank industry risk analysis: China.* New York: Standard & Poor's Bank Ratings Service.

Ghosh, D.N. 1979. *Banking policy in India: An evaluation.* Bombay: Allied Publishing.

Girardin, E. 1997. *Banking sector reform and credit control in China.* Paris: OECD Development.

Goldie-Scot, D. 1995. *Banking and finance in India.* London: FT Financial Publications.

Green, S. 2003. *China's stockmarket.* London: Profile Books.

Ho, K. 1999. *China in the WTO: A brave new world.* Hong Kong: Jardine Fleming Securities Limited.

Huang, Y. 1996. *Inflation and investment controls in China.* Cambridge: Cambridge University Press.

International Institute of Finance. 2001. *Report of the IIF Steering Committee on regulatory capital.* Washington, D.C.: International Institute of Finance.

International Monetary Fund. 2000. *International Financial Statistics.* Washington, D.C.: International Monetary Fund.

International Monetary Fund, 2001. *World Economic Outlook* (May). Washington, D.C.: International Monetary Fund.

Jadhav, N. 1994. *Monetary economics in India.* Delhi: MacMillan.

———. (Ed.). 1996. *Challenges to Indian banking: Competition, globalization, and financial markets.* Delhi: MacMillan.

Jardine Fleming: 2001. *Leading indicators, regional strategy.* Hong Kong: Jardine Fleming Securities Limited.

Joshi, V.C. and Joshi, V.V. 1998. *Managing Indian banking: The challenges ahead.* Thousand Oaks: Sage Publications.

Ju, C., Jiqui, H., and Chuntao, Y. 1981. *Nong cun jin rong.* Beijing: Zhong guo cai zheng jingji chuban she.

Kapila, R. and Kapila, U. (Eds.). 1998. *Financial sector reforms in India,* Vol. I–VI. Delhi: Academic Foundation.

Keynes, J.M. 1913. *Indian currency and finance.* London: MacMillan and Company.

Kornai, J. 1980. *Economics of shortage.* Amsterdam: North-Holland Publishing Company.

Lardy, N. 1998. *China's unfinished economic revolution.* Washington, D.C.: Brookings Institution.

Lateef, K.S. 1976. *China and India: Economic performance and prospects.* Brighton: Institute of Development Studies.

Little, I., Scitovsky, T., and Scott, M. 1970. *Industry and trade in some developing countries: A comparative study.* London: Oxford University Press.

Lou, J. 2001. *China's troubled bank loans: Workout and prevention.* The Hague: Kluwer Law International.

Maxfield, S. 1997. *Gatekeepers of growth: The international political economy of central banking in developing countries.* Princeton, New Jersey: Princeton University Press.

McKinnon, R. 1973. *Money and capital in economic development*. Washington, D.C.: Brookings Institution.

Mouskides, G. 1999. *Moody's banking system outlook: India*. New York: Moody's Investors Service.

Murty, S. (Ed.). 1997. *Financial sector reforms and economic growth in India*. Jaipur: RBSA Publishers.

Nandi, S. 1998. *Growth, financial cycles, and bank efficacy: A study of the Indian money market*. Mumbai: Business Publications.

People's Bank of China. 2000a. *China financial outlook*. Beijing: People's Bank of China.

———. 2000b. *China's financial policy and goals for financial reform*. Beijing: Information Office, People's Bank of China.

———. 1997. *Almanac of China's finance and banking*. Beijing: People's Bank of China.

Ramachandra, K.S. 1994. *Management of financial reform*. New Delhi: Anmol.

Reserve Bank of India. 2001a. *Comments of the Reserve Bank of India on the new Basel capital accord*. New Delhi: Reserve Bank of India.

———. 2001b. *Statistical tables relating to banks in India, 2000–2001*. New Delhi: Reserve Bank of India.

———. 2000a. *Statistical tables relating to banks in India, 1999–2000*. New Delhi: Reserve Bank of India.

———. 2000b. *Annual report, 1999–2000*. New Delhi: Reserve Bank of India.

———. 2000c. *Handbook of statistics on Indian economy*. Bombay: Reserve Bank of India.

Reynolds, P. 1982. *China's international banking and financial system*. New York: Praeger.

Rosen, G. 1992. *Contrasting styles of industrial reform: China and India in the 1980s*. Chicago: University of Chicago Press.

Shang, M. 1989. *Dang dai Zhonguo de jinrong shiye*. Beijing: Zhonguo she hui ke xue chuban she.

Srinivas, B. 2002. *Liberalisation and industry in India and China*. Leeds: Wisdom.

Subramanian, K. and Velayudham, T.K. (Eds). 1997. *Banking reform in India: Managing change*. New Delhi: Tata McGraw Hill Publishing Company.

Sundararajan, V. and Baliño, T. 1991. *Banking crises: Causes and issues*. Washington, D.C.: International Monetary Fund.

Swamy, S. 1973. *Economic growth in China and India, 1952–70*. Chicago: University of Chicago press.

Tam, O.K. 1999. *The development of corporate governance in China*. Northampton, Massachusetts: Edward Elgar.

———. (Ed.) 1995. *Financial reform in China*. New York: Routledge.

Tannan, M.L. 1997. *Tannan's banking law and practice in India*, Vol I–II, 19th ed. New Delhi: India Law House.

Tenev, S., Zhang, C., and Brefort, L. 2002. *Corporate governance and enterprise reform in China*. Washington, D.C.: The World Bank and the International Financial Corporation.

Tokley, I.A. and Ravn, T. 1997. *Banking law in China*. London: Sweet Maxwell.

Tong, D. 2002. *The heart of economic reform: China's banking reform and state enterprise restructuring*. Aldershot: Ashgate.

Tsai, K. 2002. *Back-alley banking: Private entrepreneurs in China*. Ithaca, New York: Cornell University Press.

Wan, T. 1999. *Development of banking law in the greater China area*. The Hague: Kluwer Law International.

Watanabe, M. 2000. *China's non-performing loan problem*. Tokyo: Institute of Developing Economies, Japan External Trade Organization.

Yang, H. 1996. *Banking and financial control in reforming planned economies*. New York: St. Martin's Press.

Yi, G. 1994. *Money, banking, and financial markets in China*. Boulder, Colorado: Westview Press.

Zhang, H. 1987. *Li shi de gui ji*. Beijing: Zhonguo jinrong chu ban she.

Zhao, H. 1985. *Huo bi yinhang gai lun*. Beijing: Jing ji ke xue shuban she.

Zhou, Z. 2001. *Chinese banking law and foreign financial institutions*. The Hague: Kluwer Law International.

Articles, Book Chapters, and Policy Papers

Agarwal, R., Inclán, C, and Leal, R. 1999. "Volatility in emerging markets." *Journal of Financial and Quantitative Analysis* 34, 33–35.

Ajit, D. and Bangar, R.D. 1998. "The role and performance of private sector banks in India, 1991–92 to 1996–97." *Political Economy Journal of India* 7, 7–20.

Akerlof, G. and Romer, P. 1993. "Looting: The Economic Underworld of Bankruptcy for Profit," *Brookings Papers on Economic Activity* 2, 1–60.

Armijo, L. and Jha, P. 1997 "Center-State Relations in India and Brazil: Privatization of Electricity and Banking." *Revísta de Economía Política* 17, 120–142.

Baekert, G. and Harvey, C.R. 1997. "Emerging equity market volatility." *Journal of Financial Economics* 43, 29–78.

Bagheri, F. and Habibi, N. 1998. "Political institutions and central bank independence: A cross-country analysis." *Public Choice* 96, 187–204.

Bailey, W. and Jagtiani, J. 1994. "Foreign ownership restrictions and stock prices in the Thai capital market." *Journal of Financial Economics* 36, 57–87.

Bank for International Settlements (BIS). 1999. "Strengthening the banking system in China: Issues and experience." BIS Policy Paper, No. 7. Basel, Switzerland: BIS.

Bardhan, P. 1971. "Recent development in Chinese and Indian agriculture." In Chen, I.K. and Uppal, J.S. (Eds.), *Comparative development of India and China*. New York: Free Press, 44–58.

Barro, R. and Gordon, D. 1983. "A positive theory of monetary policy in a natural rate model." *Journal of Monetary Economics* 12, 101–121.

Barth, J., Caprio, G., and Levine, R. 2001. "The regulation and supervision of banks around the world: A new database." Policy Research Working Paper, No. 2588. Washington, D.C.: World Bank.

Berger, H., de Haan, J., and Eijffinger, S.C.W. 2001. "Central bank independence: An update of theory and evidence." *Journal of Economic Surveys* 15, 3–40.

Berghof, E. and Roland, G. 1995. "Bank restructuring and soft budget constraints in financial transaction." Center for Economic Policy Research, Discussion Paper 1250. Washington, D.C.: Center for Economic Policy Research.

Bery, S. 1994. "Financial rehabilitation of public sector banks: Conceptual and policy aspects." *Economic and Political Weekly* 29, 251–255.

Bhalla, A.S. 2002. "Sino-Indian growth and liberalization: A survey." *Asian Survey* 42, 419–439.

———. 1995. "Recent economic reforms in China and India." *Asian Survey* 35:6, 555–572.

Bhaumik, S., Bose, S., and Coondoo, D. 2001. "The Indian bond market: A first glimpse." Centre for New and Emerging Markets Discussion Paper Series 18. London: London Business School.

Bhaumik, S. and Mukherjee, P. 2001. "The Indian banking industry: A commentary." Centre for New and Emerging Markets Discussion Paper Series 17. London: London Business School.

Bhaumik, S. and Dimova, R. 2002. "How important is ownership in a market with a level playing field: The Indian banking sector revisited." Centre for New and Emerging Markets Discussion Paper Series 24. London: London Business School.

Bhide, M.G., Prasad, A., and Ghosh, S. 2002. "Banking sector reforms: A critical overview." *Economic and Political Weekly* 37, 399–408.

Blackburn, K. and Christensen, M. 1989. "Monetary policy and policy credibility: Theories and evidence." *Journal of Economic Literature* 27, 1–45.

Blackwell, M. and Nocera, S. 1988. "Debt/Equity Swaps." IMF Working Paper WP/88/15. Washington, D.C.: International Monetary Fund.

Bonin, J.P. and Huang, Y. 2002a. "China's opening up of the banking system: Implications for domestic banks." In Ligang Song, (Ed.), *Dilemmas of China's growth in the twenty first century*. Canberra: Asia Pacific Press, 55–72.

———. 2002b. "Foreign entry into Chinese banking; Does WTO membership threaten domestic banks?" *The World Economy* 25, 1077–1093.

Brownbridge, M. 2002. "Policy lessons for prudential regulation in developing countries." *Development Policy Review* 20, 305–316.

——— and Kirkpatrick, C. 2000. "Financial regulation in developing countries." *Journal of Development Studies* 37, 1–24.

Cable, V. 1993. "The new capitalist giants: China, India, and Russia." Cedes Notes Series, No. 24. Paris: Prométhée.

Caprio, G. 1998. "Banking crises: Expensive lessons from recent financial crises." Policy Research Working Paper 1979. Washington, D.C.: World Bank Publications.

Caprio, G. 1997. "Safe and sound banking in developing countries." Policy Research Working Paper 1739. Washington, D.C.: World Bank Publications.

Caprio, G. and Klingebiel, D. 1996. "Bank insolvencies: Cross-country experience." Policy Research Working Paper 1620. Washington, D.C.: World Bank Publications.

Caprio, G. and Summers, L. 1993. "Finance and its reform: Beyond the laissez faire." Policy Research Working Paper 1171. Washington, D.C.: World Bank Publications.

Chant, J. and Pangestu, M. 1994. "An assessment of financial reform in Indonesia." In Caprio, G. Atiyas, I., and Hanson, J. (Eds.), *Financial reform: Theory and experience*. Cambridge: Cambridge University Press.

Chinn, M. and Kletzer, K. 2001. "International capital inflows, domestic financial intermediation, and financial crises under imperfect information." In Glick, R., Moreno, R., Spiegel, M. (Eds.), *Financial crises in emerging markets*. Cambridge: Cambridge University Press, pp. 196–237.

Cho, Y. and Khatkhate, D. 1989. "Lessons of financial liberalization in Asia." World Bank Discussion Papers, No. 50. Washington, D.C.: World Bank Publications.

Claessens, S. 1998. "Banking reform in transition economies." *Journal of Policy Reform* 2, 115–133.

——, Demirgüç-Kunt, A, and Huizinga, H. 2001. "How does foreign bank entry affect the domestic banking market?" *Journal of Banking and Finance* 25, 891–911.

Clarke, G., Cull, R., Martinez Peria, M.S., and Sanchez, S. 2001. "Foreign bank entry: Experience, implications for developing countries, and agenda for future research." Policy Research Working Paper 2698. Washington, D.C.: World Bank Publications.

Cull, R. and Yu, L.C. 2000. "Bureaucrats, state banks, and the efficiency of credit allocation." *Journal of Comparative Economics* 28, 1–31.

Cukierman, A. 1994. "Central bank independence and monetary control." *The Economic Journal* 104, 1437–1448.

——, Webb, S., and Neyapti, B. 1992. "Measuring the independence of central banks and its effect on policy outcomes." *World Bank Economic Review* 4, 353–398.

Dal Colle, A. 2002. "Banking in China: A view from European banks." Unpublished manuscript, School of Oriental and African Studies (SOAS).

Datar, M.K. "Redefining the debtor-creditor relationship." *Economic and Political Weekly* 37, 3786–3789.

Davies, S., 1997. "Hamstrung by their bad loans." *Financial Times*, December 8, p. 6.

De Santis, G. and İmrohoroğlu, S. 1997. "Stock returns and volatility in emerging financial markets." *Journal of International Money and Finance* 16, 561–579.

Deidda, L. and Fattouh, B. 2002. "Concentration in the banking industry and economic growth." CeFiMS, School of Oriental and Asian Studies (SOAS) Working Paper, No. DP 22. London: SOAS.

Demirgüç-Kunt, A. and Detragiache, E. 1998. "Financial liberalization and financial fragility." Policy Research Working Paper 1917. Washington, D.C.: World Bank Publications.

Demirgüç-Kunt, A. Levine, R., and Min, H.G. 1998. "Opening to foreign banks: Issues of stability, efficiency, and growth." In Proceedings of the Bank of Korea Conference on the implications of globalization of world financial markets (December).

Dewatripont, M. and Tirole, J. 1993. "Efficient governance structure: Implications for banking regulation." In Mayer, C. and Vives, X. (Eds.), *Capital markets and financial intermediation*. Cambridge: Cambridge University Press.

Dini, F. 2002. "Concentration and competition in the credit market." CeFiMS, School of Oriental and Asian Studies (SOAS) Working Paper, No. DP 27. London: SOAS.

Dixit, A. 1980. "The role of investment in entry deterrence." *Economic Journal* 90, 95–106.

Dornbusch, R. and Giavazzi, F. 1999. "Heading off China's financial crisis." In *Bank for International Settlements*, pp. 40–58.

Dossani, R. and Sáez, L. 2000. "Venture capital in India." *International Journal of Finance* 12, 1932–1946.

Drèze, J. and Saran, M. 1993. "Primary education and economic development in China and India." London School of Economics Discussion Paper DEP/47. London: London School of Economics.

Echeverri-Gent, J. 2000. "Globalization and decentralization: Lessons in good governance from China and India." Unpublished manuscript, University of Virginia, 2000.

——. and Müller, F. 1990. "The political economy of reform in three giants." In Feinberg, R., Echeverri-Gent, J., and Müller, F. (Eds.), *Economic reform in three giants: U.S. foreign policy and the U.S.S.R., China, and India*. Washington, D.C.: Overseas Development Council Publications, pp. 135–168.

Echeverri-Gent, J., Shah, A., and Thomas, S. 2001. "Reforming India's equities markets in a globalizing world." Paper Presented at the 97th Annual Meeting, American Political Science Association, San Francisco, California.

Eckaus, Richard. 1995. "The metamorphosis of giants: China and India in transition." MIT Department of Economics Working Paper No. 95/22.

Eckstein, Alexander. 1954. "Condition and prospects for economic growth in Communist China." *World Politics* 7, 1–37.

——. 1955a. "Condition and prospects for economic growth in Communist China." *World Politics* 7, 255–283.

——. 1955b. "Condition and prospects for economic growth in Communist China." *World Politics* 7, 434–447.

Edwards, S. 1984. "The order of liberalization of the external sector in developing countries." *Essays in International Finance*, No. 156. Princeton: Princeton University Press, 59–68.

Eichengreen, B. and Rose, A. 1998. "Staying afloat: External factors and emerging-market banking crises." NBER Working Paper Series No. 6370.

Eun, C. and Janakiramanan, S. 1986. "A model of international asset pricing with a constraint on the foreign equity ownership." *Journal of Finance* 41, 897–914.

Fama, E. 1980. "Agency problem and the theory of the firm." *Journal of Political Economy* 88, 288–307.

Fisher, S. 1994. "Modern central banking." In Capie, F., Goodhart, C., Fischer, S., and Schradt, N. (Eds.), *The future of central banking*. Cambridge: Cambridge University Press.

Friedman, E. and Johnson, S. 1996. "Complementarities in economic reform." *Economics of Transition* 4, 319–329.

Fry, M. 1998. "Assessing central bank independence in developing countries: Do actions speak louder than words?" *Oxford Economic Papers* 50, 512–529.

———. 1996. "Governance at the macrolevel: Assessing central bank independence in Pacific Asia and other developing areas." University of Birmingham Department of Economics, Discussion paper No. 96/27.

Geddes, B. 1991. "A game theoretic model of reform in Latin American democracies." *American Political Science Review* 85, 371–392.

Glick, R. and Hutchinson, M. 2001. "Banking and currency crises: How common are twins." In Glick, R., Moreno, R., and Spiegel, M. (Eds.), *Financial crises in emerging markets*. Cambridge: Cambridge University Press.

Grilli, V., Masciandaro, D., and Tabellini, G. 1991. "Political and monetary institutions, and public finance theories in the industrial countries." *Economic Policy* 13, 341–392.

Hanes, K. and Lindorff, D. 1998. "Can Zhu Rongji save China's banks?" *Global Finance* 12, 20–27.

Henry, P.B. 2000. "Stock market liberalization, economic reform, and emerging equity market prices." *Journal of Finance* 55, 529–564.

Holz, C. 2000. "The changing role of money in China and its implications." *Comparative Economic Studies* 42, 77–110.

———. 1992. "The role of central banking in China's economic reforms." *Cornell East Asia Series*, No. 59. Ithaca, New York.

Huang, H. and Xu, C. 1999. "Financial instability and the financial crisis in East Asia." *European Economic Review* 43, 903–914.

Islam, A. and Hilton, A. 1993. "Debt-equity swaps and development." Department of Economic and Social Development, Transnational Corporations, and Management Division. New York: United Nations.

Jensen, M. and Ruback, R. 1983. "The market for corporate control." *Journal of Financial Economics* 11, 5–50.

Jensen, M. and Meckling, W. 1976. "Theory of the firm: Management behavior, agency costs, and capital structure." *Journal of Financial Economics* 3, 305–360.

Johnston, R. and Sundararajan, V. (Eds.). 1999. "Sequencing financial sector reforms: Country experiences and issues." Washington, D.C.: International Monetary Fund.

Kaminsky, G. and Reinhart, C. 1998. "Currency and banking crises: The early warnings of distress." International Finance Discussion Paper, No. 629. Washington, D.C.: Board of Governors of the Federal Reserve System.

———. 1999. "The twin crises: The causes of banking and balance of payments problems." *American Economic Review* 89, 473–500.

Kim, E.H. and Singal, V. 2000. "Opening up of stock markets: Lessons from emerging economies." *Journal of Business* 73, 25–66.

Klapper, L. and Love, I. 2002. "Corporate governance, investor protection and performance in emerging markets." World Bank Policy Research Working Paper, No. 2818. Washington, D.C.: World Bank Press.

Klingebiel, D., Krozner, R., Laeven, L., and van Oijen, P. 2001. "Stock market responses to bank restructuring policies during the East Asian crisis." Policy Research Working Paper 2571. Washington, D.C.: World Bank Publications.

Kornai, J. 1986. "The soft budget constraint." *Kyklos* 39, 3–30.

Krueger, A. 1986. "Problems of liberalization." In Choksi, Armeane and Papageorgiou, Demetrius (Eds)., *Economic liberalization in developing countries*. London: Basil Blackwell, pp. 15–31.

Kumar, A. 1998. "Non-performing assets: No easy way out." *Capital Market* 13, 66–68.

Kydland, F. and Prescott, E. 1977. "Rules rather than discretion: The inconsistency of optimal plans." *Journal of Political Economy* 85, 473–490.

LaCroix, S., Mark, S.M., and Woo, W.T. 1999. "Anatomy of reform in two large developing countries: China and India." In Hiemenz, Ulrich (Ed.), *Growth and competition in the New World economy*. Paris: OECD Development Center.

Lal, D. 1995. "India and China: Contrasts in economic liberalization." *World Development* 23, 1475–1494.

Lardy, N. 1999. "The challenge of bank restructuring in China." In *Bank for international settlements, strengthening the banking system in China: Issues and experience*. BIS Policy Paper, No. 7. Basel, Switzerland: BIS, 17–39.

Lau, L. 1999. "The macroeconomy and reform in the banking sector in China." In *Bank for international settlements, strengthening the banking system in China: Issues and experience*. BIS Policy Paper, No. 7. Basel, Switzerland: BIS, 59–72.

Levine, R. 1999. "Foreign bank entry and capital control stabilization: Effects on growth and stability." University of Minnesota, mimeo.

Lin, J. 2002. "Is China's growth sustainable?" Center for New and Emerging Markets, London Business School, mimeo.

Lindgren, C., Garcia, G., and Saal, M. 1996. *Bank soundness and macroeconomic policy*. Washington, D.C.: International Monetary Fund.

Lo, W.C. 2001. "A retrospect in China's banking reform." *The Chinese Economy* 34, 15–28.

Lu, X. 1996. "Problems with the three lending models of China's commercial banking." *Guoji Jingrong Yanjiu* (International Financial Research), No. 12.

Malenbaum, W. 1959. "India and China: Contrasts in development performance." *American Economic Review* 49, 284–309.

———. 1956. "India and China: Development constraints." *Journal of Political Economy* 64, 1–24.

Mangano, G. 1998. "Measuring central bank independence: A tale of subjectivity and of its consequences." *Oxford Economic Papers* 50, 468–492.

Mansoob Murshed, S. and Subagjo, D. 2002. "Prudential regulation of banks in less developed economies." *Development Policy Review* 20, 247–259.

McKinnon, R. and Pill, H. 2001. "The overborrowing syndrome: Are East Asian economies different?" In Glick, R., Moreno, R., and Spiegel, M. (Eds.), *Financial crises in emerging markets*. Cambridge: Cambridge University Press, 322–355.

———. 1997. "Credible economic liberalizations and overborrowing." *American Economic Review, Papers and Proceedings* 87, 189–193.

McGregor, R. 2001. "Chinese to target scam by tourist traders." *Financial Times*, May 14, p. 13.

Mehran, H., Quintyn, M., Nordman, T., and Laurens, B. 1996. "Monetary and exchange system reforms in China." IMF Occasional Paper No. 141. Washington, D.C.: International Monetary Fund.

Michaely, M. 1986. "The timing and sequence of a trade liberalization policy." In Choksi, A. and Papageorgiou, D. (Eds.), *Economic Liberalization in Developing Countries*. London: Basil Blackwell.

Milgrom, P. and Roberts, J. 1982. "Predation, reputation and early deterrence." *Journal of Economic Theory* 27, 282–312.

Moser, P. 1999. "Checks and balances and the supply of central bank independence." *European Economic Review* 43, 1569–1593.

Mukherji, Joydeep. 1999. "China and India in 1999: Falling growth with Asian characteristics." *Standard and Poor's Credit Week*, January 13, 14–20.

Murrell, P. 1992. "Evolutionary and radical approaches to economic reform." *Economics of Planning* 25, 79–96.

Nam, S. 1994. "Korea's financial reform since the early 1980s." In Caprio, G., Atiyas, I., and Hanson, J. (Eds.), *Financial reform: Theory and experience*. Cambridge: Cambridge University Press.

Pannier, D. (Ed.). 1996. "Corporate governance and public enterprises in transitional economies." World Bank Technical Paper 323. Washington, D.C.: World Bank Publications.

Park, A. and Sehrt, K. 2001. "Tests of financial intermediation and banking reform in China." *Journal of Comparative Economics* 29, 608–644.

Pohl, G. and Claessens, S. 1994. "Banks, capital markets, and corporate governance." Policy Research Working Paper No. 1326. Washington, D.C.: World Bank Publications.

Posen, A. 1998. "Central bank independence and disinflationary stability: A missing link." *Oxford Economic Papers* 50, 335–359.

Qian, Y. and Weingast, B., 1996. "China's transition to markets: Market-preserving federalism, Chinese style." *Journal of Policy Reform* 1, 149–185.

Raj, K.N. 1983. "Agricultural growth in China and India: Role of price and non-price factors." *Economic and Political Weekly* 18, 62–75.

Rajaraman, I., Bhaumik, S., and Bhatia, N. 1999. "NPA variations across Indian commercial banking." *Economic and Political Weekly* 34, 161–168.

Rajaraman, I. and Vasishtha, G. 2002. "Non-performing loans of PSU banks: Some panel results." *Economic and Political Weekly* 37, 429–435.

Raje, P. 2000. "Where did India miss a turn in banking reform?" Center for Advanced Study of India, Occasional Paper No. 14. Philadelphia: Center for Advanced Study of India, University of Pennsylvania.

Ram Mohan, T.T. 2002. "Deregulation and performance of public sector banks." *Economic and Political Weekly* 37, 393–397.

Rangarajan, C. 1997. "Corporate governance: The new paradigm." *RBI Bulletin* 51, 787–791.

Rao, Rohit. 1999. "Collaring the crisis." *Business India*, January 11–24, pp. 50–77.

Rodrik, D. 1989. "Promises, promises: Credit policy reform via signaling." *The Economic Journal* 99, 756–772.

Rogoff, K. 1985. "The optimal degree of commitment to an intermediate monetary target." *Quarterly Journal of Economics* 100, 1169–1190.

Rosen, G. 1990. "India and China: Perspectives on contrasting styles of economic reforms." *Journal of Asian Economics* 1, 273–290.

——. 1954. "An examination of potential ling-run industrial development of India and China." *Economic Development and Cultural Change* 2, 357–370.

Rossi, M. 1999. "Financial fragility and economic performance in developing countries." IMF Working Paper 99/66. Washington, D.C.: International Monetary Fund.

Saunders, A. and Sommariva, A. 1993. "Banking sector and restructuring in Eastern Europe." *Journal of Banking and Finance* 17, 931–957.

Sáez, L. 2001. "Banking reform in China and India." *International Journal of Finance and Economics* 6, 235–244.

—— and Yang, J. 2001. "The deregulation of state-owned enterprises in India and China." *Comparative Economic Studies* 43.

Sáez, L. 1999. "India's economic liberalization, interjurisdictional competition, and development." *Contemporary South Asia* 8, 323–345.

——. 1998. "A comparison of India and China's foreign investment strategy toward energy infrastructure." *Journal of Developing Areas* 32, 199–220.

Sehrt, K. 2000. "Reevaluating fiscal federalism in the People's Republic of China: The role of banks in shaping central-local relations." Paper presented at the annual meeting of the American Political Science Association, September.

——. 1999a. "State control of urban finance: The incorporation of credit cooperatives in the PRC." Paper presented at the annual meeting of the American Political Science Association, September.

——. 1999b. "Banks vs. budgets: Credit allocation in the People's Republic of China 1984–1997." Ph.D. dissertation, Department of Political Science, University of Michigan, Ann Arbor.

Sen, A.K. 1995. "Economic development and social change: India and China in comparative perspectives." STICERD Discussion Paper No. DEP/67. London: London School of Economics.

Shirley, M. and Xu, C. 2001. "Empirical effects of performance contracts: Evidence from China." *Journal of Law, Economics, and Organization* 17, 168–200.

Shleifer, A. and Vishny, R. 1997. "A survey of corporate governance." *Journal of Finance* 52, 737–783.

Sikken, B. and de Haan, J. 1998. "Budget deficits, monetization, and central bank independence in developing countries." *Oxford Economic Papers 50, 493–511.*

Spence, A.M. 1977. "Entry, capacity, investment and oligopolistic pricing." *Bell Journal of Economics* 8, 534–544.

Srinivasan, T.N. 1990. "External sector in development: China and India 1950–1989." *American Economic Review Papers and Proceedings* 80, 113–117.

———. 1987. "Economic liberalization in China and India: Issues and an analytic framework." *Journal of Comparative Economics* 11, 427–443.

Stulz, R. 1981. "On the effects of barriers to international investment." *Journal of Finance* 36, 923–934.

Svejnar, J. 1990. "Productive efficiency and employment." In Byrd, William and Qinsong, Lin (Eds.), *China's rural industry: Structure, development, and reform.* Oxford: Oxford University Press, chapter 10.

Talwar, S. 1999. "Banking regulations and corporate governance." *RBI Bulletin* 53, 937–943.

Tan, C. 1999. "Moody's banking system outlook: China." New York: Moody's Investors Services.

"The top 1,000 world banks." 1999. *The Banker* 149.

Tong, D. 1999. "The heart of economic reform: Banking reform and state enterprise restructuring." Ph.D. dissertation, Rand Graduate School, Santa Monica, California.

Tow, C. 1999. China Construction Bank Dow Jones Interactive (April 8). Available at http://nrstg2s.djnr.com.

Wagner, H. 1999. "Central bank independence and the lessons for transition economies from developed and developing economies." *Comparative Economic Studies* 41, 1–22.

Wei, S. J. and Wang, T. 1997. "The Siamese twins: Do state-owned banks favor state-owned enterprises in China?" *China Economic Review* 8, 19–29.

Weisskopf, T. 1975. "China and India: Contrasting experiences in economic development." *American Economic Review Papers and Proceedings* 65, 356–364.

Williamson, O. 1988. "Corporate finance and corporate governance." *Journal of Finance* 43, 567–591.

Woo, W.T. 2002. "What are the legitimate worries about China's WTO membership." In Song, Ligang (Ed.), *Dilemmas of China's growth in the twenty first century.* Canberra: Asia Pacific Press, pp. 11–25.

World Bank. 2001. *Finance for growth: Policy choices in a volatile world.* Oxford: Oxford University Press.

———. 1993. *The East Asian miracle: Economic growth and public policy.* World Bank Policy Research Report. New York: Oxford University Press.

Xu, X. and Wang, Y. 1997. "Ownership structure, corporate governance, and corporate performance: The case of Chinese stock companies." Policy Research Working Paper No. 1794. Washington, D.C.: World Bank Publications.

Zhen, J. 1999. "China's reforms to take another costly decade." In *Asian Financial Markets*. Hong Kong: J.P. Morgan Securities Asia, pp. 9–18.

Zhu, M. and Huang, J. 1999. "On China's asset management corporations." *Jingji Yanjiu* (Economic Studies) 20, 3–13.

Zingales, L. 1998. "Corporate governance." In Newman, P. (Ed.), *The new Palgrave dictionary of economics and the law*. New York: Macmillan.

On-line Sources

Centurion Bank. Available at http://www.centutionbank.com.

China Minsheng Banking Corporation. Available at http://www.cmbc.com.cn.

China Orient Asset Management Company. Available at www.coamc.com.cn.

China Securities Regulatory Commission. Available at http://www.csrc.gov.cn.

Cinda Asset Management Company. Available at http://www.cinda.com.cn.

Global Trust Bank. Available at http://www.globaltrust.com.

Great Wall Asset Management Company. Available at http://www.gwamc.com.cn.

Huarong Asset Management Company. Available at http://www.huarong.com.cn.

IndusInd Bank. Available at http://www.indusind.com.

Industrial and Commercial Bank of China. Available at http://icbcasia.com.

Industrial and Development Bank of India. Available at http://www.idbi.com.

Industrial and Finance Corporation of India. Available at http://www.ifciltd.com.

Institute of International Finance. Available at http://www.iif.com.

ISI Emerging Markets. Available at http://www.securities.com.

Ministry of Finance, Government of India. Available at http://finmin.nic.in.

Reserve Bank of India. Available at http://www.rbi.org.in.

Securities and Exchange Board of India. Available at http://www.sebi.com.

Shanghai Stock Exchange. Available at http://www.sse.com.cn.

Small Industries Development Bank of India. Available at http://www.sidbi.com.

State Bank of India. Available at http://www.sbi.com.

Index